Sam in t

Cr

By Norman Cook

© Day One Publications 2006
First printed 2006

ISBN 978-1-84625-045-3

9 781846 250453 >

British Library Cataloguing in Publication Data available

Published by Day One Publications
Ryelands Road, Leominster, HR6 8NZ
☎ 01568 613 740 FAX 01568 611 473
email—sales@dayone.co.uk
web site—www.dayone.co.uk
North American—e-mail—sales@dayonebookstore.com
North American web site—www.dayonebookstore.com

Designed by Steve Devane and printed by Gutenberg Press, Malta
Illustrations by Bradley Goodwin

Contents

Foreword

B ritish soldiers in the Crimean war were at
far greater risk of dying from infectious
illnesses, such as cholera, than from battle
injuries. Conditions were atrocious and they were
in need of excellent nursing care. One source of
hope was the compassion and care shown to them
by two nurses, Florence Nightingale and Mary
Seacole. Whilst the achievements of Florence are
well known, those of Mary, the Jamaican
'doctress', have only recently become more widely
acknowledged. I certainly never heard about her
in my own nursing studies. Ironically, both were
extremely well known to the Victorian public, but
for some reason Mary Seacole became virtually
lost to history.

In schools up and down the country many
children are now learning about both of these
important nursing icons. Norman Cook is to be
congratulated for the way he brings Florence and

Mary to life. Through Sam, we can capture the dedication they both had to nursing their beloved British soldiers.

Professor Elizabeth N Anionwu, RN PhD CBE FRCN
Head of the Mary Seacole Centre for Nursing Practice, Thames Valley University
Author of ***A Short History of Mary Seacole*** (Royal College of Nursing)

The Charge of The Light Brigade

The Battle of Balaclava, 25 October 1854

Half a league, half a league,
Half a league onward,
All in the valley of Death
Rode the six hundred.
 Forward, the Light Brigade!
Charge for the guns!' he said:
Into the valley of Death
Rode the six hundred.

Forward, the Light Brigade!'
Was there a man dismay'd?
Not tho' the soldier knew
Some one had blunder'd:
Their's not to make reply,
Their's not to reason why,
Their's but to do and die:
Into the valley of Death
Rode the six hundred.

Alfred, Lord Tennyson

Chapter 1

On the streets

Sam woke with a start; not knowing how long he had slept or what had awoken him. There was no way of knowing even if it was day or night and in any case he had lost all sense of the passing of time. The dim lantern on the wooden ceiling hadn't spluttered out, plunging the tiny room into darkness, as it had often done in the past, so maybe he hadn't dozed for more than an hour or so. There it was again, a slight creaking that could almost be the straining of the ship's timbers as it ploughed through the waves.

He could also hear the wind, and the ship was tossing a little more than before his slumber. But there was something else, a sound that came at intervals, as if someone was trying to tread softly and silently to escape detection. He saw a fleeting shadow on the wall but when he turned his head there was nothing, just a dark stain on the wood. His stomach tightened and he was reminded of his hunger. He hadn't eaten properly that day. His friends Tony and Frank had been busy on deck and they were the ones who sneaked food down to him, whenever they got the chance. Still, it's my fault, he mused, I shouldn't have crept aboard without permission. There was no escaping facts, he was a criminal, a stowaway, he reflected miserably.

The boy was wide awake now, alert to the danger in the tiny cabin. He instinctively edged to his right, where he knew there was a door. The ship pitched suddenly, causing him to lurch to one side, nearly losing his balance. The howling of the wind could be heard even through the thick timbers and he sensed a storm brewing. But that was not his immediate problem. His instinct was to call loudly for help, and help might come from passing sailors but he could not bring himself to do it. Stowing away aboard ship was regarded as a serious matter by the authorities, particularly when the ship belonged to the navy. After all, he was getting a free bed, food and travel for several weeks.

If he were discovered the disgrace would not only be his, shame would also fall on his parents. They had taken a chance when they adopted him, as an orphan, three years before. Several weeks before the adoption he had been kidnapped by his uncle's criminal gang and forced to steal for them. Captain and Mrs Hopwood knew all about this, just as they knew Sam had risked his life to get a message to the police about Uncle Jack Clarke's activities. Despite what his parents knew, Sam feared they might think he had betrayed them and returned to a life of crime. They loved and trusted him so much, he couldn't bear them to think he'd let them down. He'd do anything to avoid discovery, even risk his life.

Another week and he would be in Balaclava, a coastal town on the tip of the Crimean Peninsula, part of southern Russia. His father, a captain in the army, was fighting there against the Russians in the Crimean War. Sam, afraid his father might be killed or injured, had run away from home to follow him. The short note he left for his mother said simply, 'Sorry, gone to find Papa, lots of love, Sam.' He'd felt guilty and cried bitterly as he wrote it, but the fact remained—he'd left his mother to fend for herself and his young sister.

His speed now matched that of the shadow and he reached the door. One more step and he would be free. Sam breathed a silent prayer for help then turned, facing the room, trying to identify his pursuer, when strong arms seized him from behind. A hand clasped his chest, a thumb dug into his windpipe forcing his head back, while he was frogmarched back into the cabin. He had been tricked. There were two of them, working as a team. The man who held him must have been hiding outside the room, waiting for him to leave. The other, the shadow, was there only to flush him out.

'Teddy, I got him,' called his attacker in a hoarse whisper. It was a voice Sam recognised as belonging to Razor George, a spiteful, bullying crew-member who had taken a dislike to him the minute he'd stepped aboard. A youth who Sam knew only too well as Teddy Hudson, emerged from the darkness, pushing a dagger into his belt. The young stowaway felt his heart sink. He had known Teddy and his brother, Alfie, from his early childhood in Greenwich, when both his parents were alive. Sam feared the brothers even then and his mother had warned him about the family.

'They're a bad lot, always drinking and fighting, and they'd steal the shirt from your back. You steer clear of them.' The boy knew she was right and he avoided contact as far as possible. Then, when first his mother and then his father died, leaving him all alone in the world at the age of ten, he crossed London Bridge to seek his fortune in the big city.

After living rough for a time and sleeping under the dry arch of the bridge, he had been rescued by missionary workers from the Ragged School Union. They had given him a place to sleep and provided the education he so desperately needed. He learned well and they trained him to be a shoe black at the Great Exhibition of 1851, held at the Crystal Palace in Hyde Park. He made friends and was very happy in his work, and it was there that he first met Captain (then Lieutenant) Hopwood and his wife, who later adopted him.

Unknown to Sam, Uncle Jack had also moved north of the river, along with Teddy and Alfie who worked for him as footpads. It was they who kidnapped him and introduced him to a life of crime. But Teddy was jealous and hated Sam for being Jack's nephew. Following the death of Pineapple Jack and the trial of the remaining gang members, the two brothers received the heaviest sentences because of the violence of their crimes.

They were transported to Australia and swore vengeance against the boy if they ever escaped.

Then the worst happened, Teddy had somehow broken free and then obtained a berth aboard *The Agincourt* a few weeks before Sam stowed away. And now Teddy and Razor George had somehow got together and were out to destroy him. *The Agincourt* was an old wooden sailing ship left over from the Napoleonic Wars and converted to steam for use in the modern navy. Now she was bound for the Crimea on the Black Sea with a cargo of weapons, gunpowder and mules.

'So we gotcha at last, finally caught up wiv yer.' Teddy's face was inches from Sam who had a close up view of broken, yellow teeth, a monument to a lifetime of meagre diet and poor hygiene. There was foam at the corners of Teddy's mouth and the blast of warm, putrid breath made Sam jerk his head to one side.

'I bin waitin' for yer, ever since yer done me an' Alfie,' continued Teddy. 'And directly I seen yer creepin' around the ship, all secret like wiv them two mates o' yourn, I knew me moment had come. Before it gets light, me and Razor here are chuckin' yer in the sea. And don't think of swimming for it neither, not wiv yer arms and legs tied. And no one will report yer missin', 'cos officially yer don't exist.'

Sam's mind raced. There was no doubt Teddy meant what he said. Sam had to do something quickly or he would soon be drowning in the stormy waters of the Aegean Sea. And there would be no investigation. After all there was no mention of him in official records. Not that an investigation could bring him back to life. He was in deep trouble and he had to rely on himself. His father, a former regimental wrestling champion, had taught Sam a trick or two and now was the time to use them.

The boy stopped struggling and let his body relax, forcing Razor to support all Sam's body weight with his arms. He felt the pressure on his throat reduce. The ship lurched violently as the storm gathered pace and he seized his chance. With one flowing movement he hooked a leg round his captor's standing leg and pushed his hips violently back into the body. Razor grunted, then staggered back, his head striking the oak-panelled wall behind him. He cursed horribly then slumped to the floor leaving Sam free to speed off down the passageway towards the hold. Teddy made a despairing lunge, catching Sam's ankle but the boy's strength and speed carried him clear.

He hadn't got long. George was already clambering to his feet and the boy had to find his friends quickly, otherwise he would be recaptured. The ship rolled and Sam thudded into the wooden wall of the passageway, losing his balance, then slid along on his knees. The fall took his breath away but he had to carry on. He forced himself to stand, staggered the few yards to the hold and crashed through the door, sprawling in a heap on the other side.

An overpowering smell afflicted his nostrils, the stench of more than a hundred mules in confined quarters. And a swirling mist rising from the warm bodies of the animals as well as from their urine and dung made the interior invisible. Obviously Tony and Frank had not yet started their early morning cleaning duties. Sam stood up and edged forward a few feet, making for the hammocks where his friends slept. He felt safer now, as he must be invisible to anyone at the door. His eyes felt as if they were on fire and tears flowed despite his efforts at self-control. He began to cough and reaching into his pocket he pulled out a large handkerchief, which he tied round his mouth as a crude filter. He'd always marvelled that anyone could possibly sleep in the choking atmosphere of the hold. Then there was the noise. The whinnying, snorting and neighing of all those mules made rest all but impossible.

Sam could now see the light from an oil lamp in the corner of the hold and there, standing shovel in hand, he could make out the outline of Tony. Sam breathed a sigh of relief, his prayer for help had been answered. The fair-haired young seaman looked up. 'Sam, what are you doing here at this hour? Don't you know you could be discovered by the morning watch?'

'Of course I know Tony, I'm not daft. But they're after me, the two I told you about, Teddy and Razor George. They might be here, in the hold, right now,' whispered Sam hoarsely through the handkerchief.

Tony picked up a pitchfork, a grim smile on his face. 'Then we'd better be ready for them, hadn't we?' Tony was a relaxed, carefree sort of fellow but at well over six foot and powerfully built, even the strongest sailor thought twice before getting on the wrong side of him. Sam looked at the broad chest and thick tattooed forearms, and felt reassured.

He recalled the day, just a few weeks back, when he first climbed the gangplank with his donkey, Carrots. He wanted to find his father at all costs and had a vague idea of bluffing his way on board, but before he had a chance one of the ratings turned awkward and barred his way.

'What's that thing you got there, you don't call it a mule, do yer?' sneered the man who Sam later knew as Razor George. 'It's too small for a start. You couldn't call it a donkey even, more like a rat if you ask me.' He turned to a group of cronies and grinned. One or two jeered and catcalled their approval and waited to see what would happen next.

That was enough for Carrots but whether it was the tone of voice or the swaggering attitude that infuriated him, Sam never knew. All he heard was the donkey snort, then he put his head down and charged, sending Razor sprawling onto his back, before scuttling away like a frightened spider into the darkness of the lower decks.

Carrots was a donkey of unyielding likes and dislikes, an animal of stubborn disposition who loved his friends just as he hated his enemies. And enemies ranged from anyone who tried to fob him off with inferior, non-carrot-like vegetables, to loud and aggressive people. You couldn't call him a handsome donkey by any means. For a start he had a withered ear, the result of an accident when he was just a foal. Then there was the look on his face, a kind of sulky, grumpy look, as if he were out of sorts with the world. His fur was a rich brown but from close up it had a moth-eaten appearance. But what Carrots lacked in beauty he more than made up for in character.

'Need any help, young 'un?' Sam heard a voice from one of a knot of sailors leaning over the ship's rail. 'Only I don't trust 'im,' said a pleasant, fair-haired young man who was smiling across at him. 'I'd watch myself from now on if I were you, 'e's not one to get on the wrong side of.' He nodded at the stairway where Razor had disappeared. Later the boy was to realise to his cost how right the stranger had been.

By now Sam had had time to take stock of the open, friendly face and he decided things were so desperate that swift action was required. After all, the rumpus must have attracted the attention of quite a few people, so he did the only thing he could, he confided in the young man.

'My father's fighting in the Crimea, he's in the army, you see sir and I want to join him,' said Sam nervously.

'So you've enlisted on *The Agincourt*. What a good idea, I like a lad with spirit. And they've let you bring your donkey. Unusual, though, the Navy isn't normally that generous and by the way, no need to call me sir. Tony's the name.' He reached out and shook Sam warmly by the hand.

'Mine's Sam and well sir, er, Tony I haven't enlisted at all and that's the problem,' said the boy feeling for the first time that he should have stayed at home in Blackwall by the Thames.

Tony's face fell. 'Haven't enlisted, so you want to be a stowaway. But how do you think you're going to get away with it? The voyage will take at least three weeks and you've nothing to live on, let alone anywhere to sleep.' He was joined by a stocky, dark-haired fellow who beamed at Sam.

'I couldn't help overhearing some of what the boy here was saying,' said the other. 'Sam is it?'

Sam smiled assent and the other continued. 'You haven't forgotten by any chance that I was a stowaway once, have you Tony, and you helped me? Sam looks an honest lad and I think we ought to help him find his father.'

'It's not an easy one this, I need time to think. I'll be back in a minute.' Tony strode off and the boy saw him at the far end of the ship, leaning over the side. The dark-haired sailor smiled reassuringly and they waited. Just as Sam was beginning to think he had been abandoned, Tony returned.

He was silent for a moment and then nodded. 'Very well Frank, I expect we can find him somewhere to sleep and he can share our food. We should be able to keep him hidden easily enough. After all, we'll be there in less than a month.' Sam gave a sigh of relief. And the two proved as good as their word, acting both as protectors and friends, and finding a berth for Carrots among the mules.

From where he stood Sam saw two figures emerging from the mist. Teddy and Razor had found him.

'Right 'and 'im over, he belongs to us,' said Teddy in a voice that both whined and threatened at the same time. He raised a heavy, gnarled piece of wood and took a step towards Tony. George, a small rat-like man with a shaven head and a hard, merciless stare, brandished the weapon that had given him his nickname, a sharp cut-throat razor.

'You're not taking him anywhere, said Tony directing the pitchfork prongs at Teddy. 'And remember, we're not alone.' He glanced meaningfully behind the two rogues.

'I suppose you fink we was born yesterday,' snarled Razor in a hoarse voice. 'That's the oldest trick in the boo ...' The villain broke off in mid-sentence as a heavy leather feeding bag, wielded by Frank, crashed into the side of his head. The man groaned then sprawled senseless among the mule dung and wet straw. With perfect timing, at the precise moment the bag hit George, Jack leapt forward with the pitchfork, surprising Teddy and pinning him to a wooden pillar, the twin prongs either side of his throat.

The young rogue blinked nervously and gulped. 'Whatcha gonna do to me, you ain't gonna kill me or nuffink, are yer?' he began to sob. How different he looks, thought Sam, like a frightened child now the tables have been turned.

'Quiet you scoundrel or you might end up in the sea just as you'd have done with young Sam here,' shouted Tony angrily and Teddy subsided, red faced, snivelling softly.

'What do we do with them now,' said Sam anxiously, 'we can't really throw them in the sea, can we?'

'I think I've got a plan,' said Tony, 'but first we

need to tie them up with those leather straps we use for mule tethers.' Soon the two scoundrels were securely bound, gagged and hidden out of sight behind a huge pile of straw.

'No one will find them there,' said Tony as he outlined his idea. 'Tomorrow morning we reach Constantinople and I have to buy feed for the mules in the market. We can hide these two on the cart and take them to the British Embassy. We'll use Carrots; I expect he'll enjoy a run out.'

'But I can't go to the Embassy,' said Sam. 'They might ask questions and find I'm not listed among the crew.'

'He's right you know,' said Frank. 'We've got to be careful otherwise Sam might get caught along with those two. I think we'd do better to leave them tied up on the Embassy steps with notices pinned to them, explaining what they've done and saying that Teddy is an escaped transport.'

Tony looked thoughtful. 'Yes, I think that's all we can do but I think we've got to realise that George may get away with it. A notice pinned to him is hardly proof of guilt.'

'But they should make enquiries about Teddy and send him back to Australia. And I don't suppose George will be back by the time we sail,' said Frank.

And so it was that at daybreak the next morning, the donkey cart left the ship with Sam and the two prisoners hidden under tarpaulins. Directly they turned the corner and could no longer be seen from *The Agincourt*, Tony shouted to Sam, who sat up and looked around. The wriggling forms of Teddy and Razor George were still under the covers making frantic attempts to escape. Frank was with Tony on the driving seat and the rising sun could be seen through the masts and rigging of the ships in harbour. Daylight was coming to the streets of Constantinople.

Despite the early hour, there were plenty of passers-by, mostly men clad in baggy trousers, blouses and the flower-pot-shaped hat, known as the fez. Sam stared in wonder as a drover with a train of camels behind him appeared from a narrow side street and headed for the docks. Up till now he had only seen pictures of the great beasts in schoolbooks. On the skyline he saw several domes with tall towers next to them and Frank told him these were Moslem temples, known as mosques, and the towers were minarets.

They passed through a large, evil-smelling region of narrow, winding streets piled high with rubbish. In places knots of men had gathered in small groups and some looked at the cart with a kind of menacing curiosity. The whole area made Sam nervous and he was glad when they reached a broad highway where the air was fresh.

'Over there Sam, what do you think of that?' the boy heard Tony say, and he turned to see a vast white building. 'That's the Cathedral of Saint Sophia, one of the most famous buildings in the world. Actually, strictly speaking it's not a cathedral any more, it's a mosque. We're not far from the Embassy now.'

A short distance away Sam could see a Union Flag flying over a large mansion. He felt excitement rise at the sight of a small piece of Britain in a strange land, and then he sighed as it made him think of his mother and home. The two great wooden doors at the front and a brass plaque indicated the main entrance, and there were no guards, at least not from the outside.

'If we're quick, we can drop these two off and get away before the staff inside even notice,' said Tony, looking down at the writhing forms of Teddy and Razor George. Notices detailing their crimes were pinned to their jackets and soon they were propped up in sitting positions on the Embassy steps. Tony and Frank ran back, jumped on the cart and Sam, who was driving, urged Carrots quickly away. As they turned the corner, the boy saw the doors open and the donkey emitted a triumphal bray of delight.

A few days later *The Agincourt* had crossed the Black Sea and was entering the small Crimean port of Balaclava. Sam watched from a tiny porthole in the hold as his two companions made the mules ready for the short trip ashore. The harbour was very narrow and the boy wondered how they could possibly reach their moorings without colliding with other ships already docked. There were craft of every shape and size, from noble British steamers to small rowing boats. Because the land on three of the sides consisted of steep hills, they seemed to be sailing through a small basin full of sea water. It was a gusty day and each time the wind blew the jungle of masts swayed in unison like the trees in Epping Forest on a stormy day.

The boy glanced at himself in the mirror and paused for a moment. One thing was certain, his fair hair had grown long on board ship and it could do with a wash. And although he still had the big blue eyes of childhood, now, at nearly fourteen years of age, his face was definitely longer and more manly.

They were in the act of docking in a strange land and Sam no longer understood his own emotions. On the one hand he was happy and excited at the thought of finding his father, yet he was also fearful because soldiers could be wounded or even killed in battle. And always at the back of his mind there was fear of rejection, followed by a speedy return home in shame.

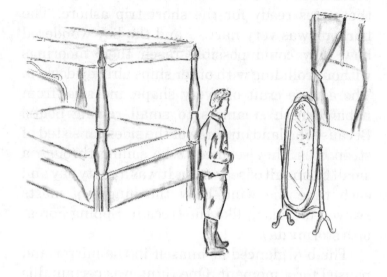

Chapter 2

Balaclava

The donkey cart rattled along the quayside of the small town of Balaclava and Sam felt at peace with the world. The worries that gripped him at the end of the voyage had lifted as soon as he was free of the confines of the ship. It was mid-October but the sun felt warm on his skin and life was good.

Carrots was lively too, almost playful after his release from the ship, and Sam could understand why. It was wonderful to breathe fresh air after the awful, choking atmosphere of the hold and the donkey showed it in his bearing. With head held high he trotted along in a jaunty manner snorting in delight at the sights and sounds of the town.

He even eeyored sociably at a line of mules being led along the harbour road by a group of soldiers. Normally he hated mules and aboard ship had stood eyeball to eyeball, for fully five minutes, with one large aggressive animal who tried to jostle him away from the feeding trough. Eventually the mule, the head of the herd, blinked first and that was his big mistake because Carrots, ever the opportunist, lowered his head, charged and butted him out of the way. From that time forth Carrots always fed first. Actually Sam, who had seen the whole incident, had foreseen the outcome right from the word go. He always reckoned that with the right guidance Carrots could have been eyeballing champion of the British Empire.

The dockside at Balaclava lacked the large warehouses that were a feature of the London docks, near to Sam's home at Blackwall by the

Thames. Instead, much of the freight unloaded from the ships was stacked in the open, in vast chaotic piles, until someone from the army claimed it. As a result theft was a way of life for some and the town drew criminals like iron filings to a magnet. In the local drinking dens shady characters from all over Eastern Europe spent their days plotting and scheming. The few huts built along the waterside had been commandeered by the military to administer the movements of both goods and personnel. It was a busy, bustling place where the noisy, boisterous servicemen of the Allied armies and navies greatly outnumbered the locals.

On board *The Agincourt* Tony had told Sam all about the railway being built by British engineers, and he came upon it almost at once. Not that it was difficult to find, since the terminus was situated close to the docks for ease of transportation. A party of redcoats was busy loading guns onto waggons that soon would be bound for the battlefront.

The actual town of Balaclava could be seen up on the steep, rocky hills that circled the harbour. From his position near the docks, Sam could see a white church with a golden dome that was shaped like an onion. The church was surrounded by a cluster of low, red-roofed houses and on the higher slopes were a number of ancient stone forts. It all looked so romantic, almost like a true-life fairy tale village, and he promised himself he would go exploring as soon as he had the chance.

As they approached the outskirts of the town, Sam spied a grassy field with a pond and he pulled off the road to give Carrots a rest. He unhitched the donkey, who promptly wandered across to slake his thirst. Sam then reclined on his seat and sighed contentedly. They were alone apart from a bare-foot peasant lad who was busy skimming stones across the water. For a few moments the English boy stretched, arched his back, closed his eyes and let the golden sunlight beat down on his eyelids. Almost without noticing he found himself singing a jaunty sea shanty he'd learnt from Tony and Frank.

'I'll put on my boots and I'll blow the man down,
    Way, hey, blow the man down.
I'll put on my boots and I'll blow the man down,
    Gimme some time to blow the man down.'

'Way, hey, blow the man down.' Sam sat up and looked around. Someone had cut in on his song but there was no one about. No one, that is, apart from the young peasant. And a local peasant couldn't possibly be singing in English.

Suddenly the boy looked up and laughed. 'Hey English, you like my song?' And so saying he swaggered across to where the English boy was sitting. He was a little younger than Sam, about twelve or thirteen perhaps, shorter and more slightly built. A year or so back Sam too had been slender but the good food served at the Hopwood's had filled him out and broadened his shoulders. The youngster's hair, jet-black tight curls, topped a thin elfin face that was both brown and weather-beaten. A coarse cloth jacket was held together by a length of rope instead of buttons.

'But how did you learn English,' stammered Sam at length, hardly knowing what to say. 'Did they teach you at school?'

The boy laughed uproariously and then turned several cartwheels, causing the battered peak cap, worn rakishly on the back of his head, to tumble into the dust. 'School, English? My people do not go to school,' he chuckled, as he brushed the dirt off the cap. 'I learn from British soldiers. My people see great army land at Eupatoria and then march south. We follow and I get to know soldiers. We watch Russians try to stop Allies at Alma River but Allies win. I help British with wounded and they give me gumbugs. Have gumbug English.'

The Allies were the combined armies of Turkey, France and Britain. Sam took a black-and-white sweet from the bag and popped it into his mouth. 'Thank you, and by the way the word is humbug. And what is your name?'

'Name is Ishmael. Your name English?'

'Samuel, but call me Sam.'

'I call you Sam, English. Gumbug good?'

'Delicious, thank you very much. But who are your people? Aren't you a Russian?'

'My people are Romany. How you say, Gypsy? Russians not like Gypsies. Cossacks come with swords and kill my people.' Ishmael spat. Then his smile returned. 'At Alma River, Allies fire guns, boom, boom and Cossacks run.' He laughed, did a handstand, walked around on his hands for a short distance, then deftly jumped to his feet. 'You like to come and see my people?'

Sam thought quickly. The truth is he had a problem. He had followed his father thousands of miles and now he didn't have the least idea what to do. He knew that if he confronted Captain Hopwood straight away the Captain would ship him home without hesitation.

So Tony and Frank, who had contacts, had gone to the British Army camp to find Sam work until the time was ripe to tell his father. Of course he had no idea when that would be. Neither could he think of any situation where he could possibly contact him without being sent home in disgrace. All Sam could do was to take one step at a time and hope for the best. So he had arranged to meet his two friends upon their return in the late afternoon. And the meeting was vital because without work he could not survive. They would be leaving the Crimea as soon as *The Agincourt* sailed and then he was on his own, without friends, in a strange land.

'I'd love to come, Ishmael, but you must promise that I'll be back before nightfall. I have friends to meet.'

The gypsy boy gave a mischievous grin and promptly performed two cartwheels to show his pleasure. Sam warmed to a smile made more striking by the contrast between Ishmael's snow-white teeth and his swarthy features.

'Up the hill, English,' shouted Ishmael joyously. 'I show you the way.'

They headed for the domed church and the low houses, except that when they got there, everything appeared different. The church needed a coat of paint and the tumbledown houses were as shabby as the peasants who lived in them. On closer inspection the fairy tale evaporated to expose the grim reality of everyday life in the Crimea.

On the way to the heights they passed the forts, as poorly kept as the houses and church. The way was steep and Carrots began to tire before they reached the top but the stubborn donkey made it without stopping, just as Sam knew he would. But he needed a rest so Sam paused at the top just long enough for Ishmael to feed the donkey his favourite dish of carrots. Sam was pleased to note that the Gypsy and the donkey hit it off straight away.

As the boy looked down from the heights above Balaclava, the spectacle filled him with wonder and for several minutes he simply stared, oblivious to his surroundings.

'You like the view, hey English?' Ishmael's voice aroused him from his daydream and he glanced around. Carrots was grazing contentedly and all seemed right with the world.

'The ships down in Balaclava Harbour, they look like toys and the Black Sea, it's so blue,' said Sam in awe.

'What's black but blue English?' guffawed Ishmael, who then rolled on the ground in a fit of uncontrollable laughter. 'The Romany people watch as Allies take Balaclava,' he said at length when he recovered himself. 'We very pleased and then the Royal Navy use it to bring guns from across the sea. Balaclava very important. No Balaclava, no war.'

Sam was impressed at the depth of Ishmael's knowledge. Tony and Frank had already explained the importance of the town as a supply centre for the Allied armies besieging the naval port of Sebastopol. But the Gypsy boy had already worked it out for himself, or perhaps the elders of his family had.

'Over there, English, is Sebastopol,' said Ishmael, seeming to pick up Sam's thoughts as he pointed out the fortified town. You could see ships of the Russian Navy quite clearly in the harbour on the far side. The object of the war was for the Allies to take Sebastopol because once the Russian Black Sea fleet was captured or destroyed, it could no longer attack the Turkish Empire. There were Turkish colonies around the Black Sea and only three hundred miles to the south of the Crimea was Turkey itself. Britain and France feared Russian strength if she managed to defeat Turkey.

'Kadikoi,' said Ishmael, pointing out a nearby village. 'British Headquarters near Kadikoi, so British engineers build road and railway from Balaclava to there. Then they carry on building till they reach Sebastopol.' Sam could see a concentration of army tents near the village. He could also make out a marching column of tiny red-coated soldiers.

There was a biting October wind up there on the hilltop and Sam began to shiver. 'We move on, English,' said Ishmael, reading the signs of discomfort. Carrots pulled the cart along a narrow, rutted track for several miles before the Gypsy directed them across open country. The high landscape was bleak and almost bare of trees but they seemed to be headed for a small wood, the only one within his range of vision. The ground was uneven and on one occasion a wheel went into a ditch, catapulting Ishmael onto his back in muddy water. He was back on his feet in an instant, laughing and joking, but after that Sam drove more carefully. Just before the wood stood a large rock, where Ishmael gave a loud whistle. A shadow on top moved and the Romany boy signalled with his hand.

'We Gypsies have to be careful it's not Cossacks, English. Anyway, we're here now,' said Ishmael.

Sam saw Romany waggons, many beautifully painted, positioned among the trees. They arrived at a muddy clearing where men stood talking by a blazing fire and women tended a large cooking pot. Ishmael jumped down, ran to the men and they engaged in animated conversation. Then he pointed to Sam and one of the men strode across to the cart with him.

'English, this is my father, Amos.' Sam left the cart and reached forward to shake hands, only to be surrounded by a pack of snarling dogs. Eventually, after much yelling by Amos and Ishmael, they calmed down but continued to sniff suspiciously round the stranger's legs. 'Sorry English, but the dogs don't like visitors, we train them to chase people away. Now they like you, though,' Ishmael smiled. Amos was an older, greyer version of his son, and he shook Sam's hand warmly, making a little speech in the Romany tongue.

'Amos say sorry he cannot speak English. We Romanies are a wandering people and he does speak Russian, Turkish and Romanian. He say you are a good *gorjo*,' laughed Ishmael.

'*Gorjo*, what on earth is that? enquired Sam.

'Means you are not Gypsy, English,' said his friend who was joined by a round, jolly woman in the kind of dark, ankle-length dress favoured by all those clustered about the pot. A blushing young girl with black curly hair and ragged clothes clung to her skirts.

'English, you must meet my mother Hannah and my sister Mireli.' The woman said nothing but threw her arms round Sam and crushed him to her bosom. After disentangling himself, with both he and Hannah giggling helplessly, he held out his hand to Mireli. The little girl, however, shyly declined to shake and ran off to play with the dogs and the other children.

'My mother and my sister like you,' said Ishmael, 'I can tell. And my father wants you to stay to dinner.'

The meal was a stew, probably rabbit, guessed Sam and the atmosphere around the camp fire became cosy and friendly as the Romanies swapped jokes and stories among themselves. With Ishmael translating, Amos told Sam how, long ago the Gypsies had left their native land with its elephants, tigers and temples to travel the world. He also explained that the Romanies now made their living mainly by trading horses and that Cossack patrols often tried to steal them. The Gypsies were very poor, Sam could see that, and the camp was a dirty, dusty place. But the living quarters, in the painted waggons, were spotlessly clean.

The stew was so delicious and the conversation flowed so easily, that Sam quite forgot the time. Before he realised, the bright sunshine of the October day had given way to twilight. Then he was aware of a certain unease gnawing away at him. He pushed the feeling to the back of his mind but it bobbed back, stronger than ever. And then it hit him. Guilt, he felt guilty because he had forgotten his meeting with Tony and Frank.

Sam leapt to his feet and beckoned Ishmael to the shadow lands round the campfire. 'Ishmael, I don't know what to do, I have to be back quickly to meet my friends. They may have found me work and I don't know the way to Balaclava.' Sam could have kicked himself for being so selfish. He had neglected his friends just for a few hours enjoyment.

'Don't worry English, I get you there double quick. I know short wound,' said Ishmael.

'You mean short cut,' laughed Sam.

Ishmael laughed and walked around on his hands to amuse the younger children, who giggled helplessly and tried to copy him. 'I tell my people Sam says goodbye, then we go.'

They left the camp at breakneck speed with Ishmael and Mireli hanging on the back. Afterwards, Sam's memory of the journey back was somewhat hazy but he did remember travelling along a narrow track, scarcely wide enough for a footpath, and nearly turning over several times.

'Faster, English, faster,' yelled the two Romany children, in excited voices. And to make things worse, Carrots caught the reckless mood, cutting corners in a dangerous manner, particularly on the steep streets leading down from the heights to the harbour.

Tony was pacing up and down, looking at his pocket watch, while Frank sat patiently on an old beer barrel when Sam arrived. 'Sorry I'm late,' called Sam nervously, hoping his friends weren't too angry.

'I'm surprised you're here at all, actually,' said Tony in reasonable tones. 'When we left you, I said to Frank, "The quayside in this town is like a maze. We'll be lucky if we see him before next week." ' Frank and Tony exchanged winks and he knew his friends had forgiven him. He turned to introduce Ishmael and Mireli but they'd gone, melted away into the darkness.

'Well, we had a good day, much better than we expected,' said Frank. 'Our recruiting sergeant friend couldn't help but he passed us on to the Hospital Conveyance Corps. Their job is to drive the waggons that take wounded soldiers away from the battlefield. They also help with their treatment and drive them to hospital if necessary. We've arranged for you to meet a Sergeant Edwards, first thing tomorrow up at the British camp.'

'And what's more, we've got news of your father,' beamed Tony. 'A Captain Hopwood has transferred from his old regiment to the 11th Hussars and been promoted to colonel at the same time. Not bad, eh, young 'un?'

'Not bad? It's bloomin' marvellous,' yelled Sam excitedly. 'He was only a lieutenant when they adopted me. Then he became a captain for volunteering to fight in the Crimea. And now he's a colonel. Soon he'll be a general.'

At seven the next morning Sam was on the military road to Kadikoi bound for the British camp. Despite the early hour it was already thronged with all manner of folk going about their business. At one point he and a squad of British cavalry were forced to take to the grass verge because a broken ox cart had blocked the progress of a gigantic cannon bound for the front.

By nine o'clock he had arrived and was talking

to Sergeant Edwards, a tall, powerful man with a barrel chest and waxed moustaches. To Sam's surprise he was offered a position straight away, with no questions asked.

'To be frank with you, the army has taken on three hundred men for the Hospital Conveyance Corps and hardly any are up to the job. You see, they are mostly Chelsea Pensioners, so I'm looking for some young blood to liven things up a bit,' said the sergeant.

'But I've no idea what to do, I've never even tied a bandage,' protested Sam.

'It's not a problem, son,' said the kindly sergeant. 'You can work with old Joe Harrison, he's a man with many years of experience. And by the way, we're using some special new wagons, the latest thing out. They're known as ambulances.' He indicated a sturdy vehicle with four compartments situated at the rear. Each compartment held a stretcher for carrying the wounded. 'But you can carry on using your donkey cart till you're properly trained.'

Joe Harrison was a frail gentleman in his early sixties, with a wisp of white hair carefully combed across the top of his bald head. He was about two inches shorter than Sam, which made him about five feet two. As a boy soldier he'd fought in Spain for Wellington's Peninsular Army, in the years before the Battle of Waterloo.

Old Joe showed Sam his sleeping quarters, a few feet of space in a tent, then took him to the store to fit him out with a uniform. The boy hadn't changed his clothes since he had left London a month ago and it was a relief to be rid of his ragged old shirt and trousers.

Sam whistled in appreciation of the new outfit. 'Very nice, Joe, smart grey jacket with silver buttons and matching breeches. Just what the doctor ordered.'

'And them shoes o' yourn 'ave seen better days. I'll sort you out a strong pair of army boots.'

An excited Sam put the new clothes on and stood squinting at himself in front of the mirror, bottoning and unbuttoning his jacket and smoothing his trousers till he was satisfied with his appearance. Joe laughed out loud, speaking to no one in particular. 'Look at him, staring at his own reflection. He won't be standing around admiring himself when the Russian guns start to fire.'

Sergeant Edwards appeared and adjusted the angle of Sam's pillbox hat. 'Don't you worry, he's a good lad, he'll soon learn, Private Harrison. 'Now, Private Hopwood,' he said, turning to the boy, 'there's a job that needs doing urgently. I want you two to deliver a parcel to the Military Hospital in Balaclava. It has to be there by this afternoon. Don't bother to come back tonight, they'll find you a bed. But make sure you're back for ambulance training by ten o'clock tomorrow morning.' Sam felt his cheeks flush with pride at the use of the military title. He was a soldier at last, just like his father.

And so it was that the odd couple, a retired soldier and a novice ambulance boy found themselves on the outskirts of Balaclava, at the Church of Kadikoi, newly converted to an army hospital. In the morning they would rise early and return to the army camp.

Chapter 3

The Light Cavalry Brigade

Shortly after daybreak, Sam and Joe left the hospital and headed back, but it wasn't until they left Kadikoi that events took an unexpected turn. Under Joe's directions they had intended turning off the road and taking a short cut along a little known track that led back to the British Camp. But Joe was hazy about the route and soon they got lost. Suddenly there was a sound of shouting and a group of soldiers came running towards them over the brow of a hill.

'Turks, Sam, look at them fezzes,' said Joe. Sam eased the cart to one side to allow them past and having ignored the pair completely, the troopers disappeared into the distance.

'I reckon they're headed for Kadikoi or even Balaclava. I wonder what the hurry is,' said Sam in puzzled tones. Within minutes a large body of cavalrymen, dressed in blue greatcoats, came into view.

'Blimey, Sam, them are Russians, we'd better take cover before they spot us,' said Joe.

Sam reined Carrots in behind a nearby line of trees and both he and Joe stood stock still, hardly daring to breathe as the horsemen sped past in a long ragged line, their attention directed on the road ahead. 'There's enough of 'em and they must be after the Turks. There ain't much of a garrison in Balaclava and I reckon that's what the Russians are after. You know, taking the town, and if that happens we're all done for,' gulped the old man.

'I think we need to make a move and get back to camp as soon as possible,' said Sam, who felt distinctly ill at ease. They set off again to the thunder of artillery coming from somewhere ahead.

Joe looked around him. 'Hold on I think I know where we are. That's Canrobert's Hill way over there on the right. I reckon we're just coming up to North Valley.' Sam felt relieved; at least they could get back and report to Sergeant Edwards.

An infantry troop was marching directly in front of them and Sam shouted across to the officer to ask what was happening. 'It's the Russians, more than twenty thousand infantry, so I've heard, marching on Balaclava,' shouted the man. 'The Turks were guarding the heights outside the town and the Russians have turfed them out. There's going to be a battle and I suggest you and the old boy keep out of harm's way,' he sneered.

Joe chose to ignore the contempt in the other's voice. 'I thought it might be something like that,' he whispered to Sam. 'We ain't got much time but I still reckon we can make it if we hurry.'

They crossed a road and turned right to avoid some French soldiers, because neither could speak French and they didn't want to be challenged.

'Blimey Sam, there's some Russians right in front of us. Pull in to them bushes,' hissed Joe. The boy did as he was told, taking care to keep Carrots out of sight in the sparse cover offered by the shrubs. Then he climbed down from the cart and followed Joe who was crawling on his stomach to the edge of the thicket.

'Up there on the hill to our left, some Russian infantry. Sam looked and saw that his companion was correct. The troopers wore the same kind of blue greatcoats as the cavalry they'd seen earlier. 'Crikey,' shouted Joe becoming hysterical. 'See that old boy up on the hill to the right. Well that's old Raglan, he's our Commander in Chief. We're stuck right between the British and the Russians. I ain't moving, I'm staying put.'

'But we've got to move,' roared Sam defiantly. 'It's our duty to join the Allies,' and he gave Carrots a tug. But the stubborn donkey refused to move. He'd dug in his hooves, so to speak, and was going no further. Now there was no choice. They had to stay.

'That donkey's got a lot more sense than you,' laughed Joe. They put their heads down as a shell whistled overhead. 'Wait a minute, that's the Heavy Brigade in action,' said Joe a little later as he peered through the long grass.

A line of scarlet-coated British cavalry was charging uphill towards a very much larger Russian force. The two groups of horsemen grappled in hand-to-hand combat and the lines of swayed to and fro for what must have been several minutes, with neither side gaining the advantage. The enemy numbers were so huge that Sam feared the Heavy Brigade would be overwhelmed. But it was the Russians who started to give ground, slowly at first and then quite suddenly they were in retreat, fleeing the conflict. The boy felt a glow of pride that British soldiers had fought so well and felt reassured that his father would be safe in battle with such comrades.

'I think I've worked out what's happened,' said Joe. 'The Russians are in control of the redoubts. As the man said, they took 'em from the Turks this mornin' and that's why we saw the Turks runnin'.'

'Redoubts, what are they? I never heard of 'em,' said Sam.

'They're a kind of primitive fort, made of earthworks. Up there on the hill in front of us. They were built to defend Balaclava and now we've lost 'em. Old Raglan must've been using the Heavy Brigade to get 'em back. Trouble is they didn't succeed. They chased the Russian cavalry off but they didn't take the redoubts. He'll try again though, I bet he's got a trick or two up 'is sleeve,' replied Joe.

'There's something going on up there; Lord Raglan's talking to somebody,' said Sam.

'I reckon that's Sir Richard Airey,' said Joe, after careful thought. 'He writes down the orders as the Chief gives 'em. I think that's what he's doin' now. And when he's finished he'll pass it on to Captain Nolan of the 15th Hussars, whose job it is to take it to the battlefield commanders.'

'If the young man in the red and gold is Captain Nolan, then he's on his way down the slope now,' said Sam.

The old man and the boy watched spellbound as the order was passed on to one commander, who seemed to be arguing violently with Nolan over it. The order then went to a cavalry officer and another argument ensued.

'That cavalry officer is Lord Cardigan of the 11th Hussars, I've seen him before,' said Joe. 'He's in charge of the Light Cavalry Brigade.'

'What a coincidence!' yelled Sam excitedly. 'My father, Colonel Hopwood, has just transferred to the 11th Hussars.'

'I reckon Old Raglan wants them to take the redoubts,' said Joe. 'That's where Nolan was pointing. I think something's happening; looks like the Light Cavalry Brigade are about to go into battle.'

From their hiding place the two could see the Light Brigade beginning to advance along the North Valley. The two companions flattened themselves into the bushes and kept their heads down. The leading riders were just yards away as they increased speed to a trot and the riding tackle jangled as if to signal the change of pace. Sam felt the ground vibrate under the pounding of hundreds of horses. The boy caught a warm horsey smell as the brigade passed and he could clearly see steam rising from the flanks of the animals. Clods of turf were being thrown into the air as the hooves churned up the earth.

Suddenly a figure in a red and gold uniform was riding diagonally across the path of the brigade, shouting and waving his sword and pointing at the redoubts on top of the heights.

'That's Captain Nolan. Somethin's gone wrong, boy. I reckon that fool Cardigan thinks he's got to charge the Russian guns at the far end of the valley. And Nolan's trying to put him right,' said Joe thoughtfully. Nolan may well have succeeded but for a volley of shots from the Russians. The young man screamed in pain and dropped his sword, pierced to the heart by a piece of shrapnel.

The Light Brigade continued advancing in three lines with Lord Cardigan leading from the front. He may have been a fool but he was a brave one. And he was no youngster either; Sam estimated him to be in his fifties. The boy continued to scan the ranks of soldiers anxiously until he found what he was looking for; his father was in the second line on the left flank and so was on the side nearest him. His heart leapt for joy. How handsome he looks, how glorious riding his great black charger, sabre in hand, thought Sam. Colonel Hopwood was a square-shouldered,

strongly built man, clean-shaven with flashing
blue eyes. His splendid form was perfectly set off
by the cherry-red trousers and the blue-and-gold
jacket of the 11th Hussars. Sam felt a glow of pride
in the man who meant so much to him, who had
rescued him from a life of crime on the streets.
Suddenly the sunlight reflecting off the raised
sabre made the sword glitter in his father's hands.
Then, as if by a signal, the morning sun caught the
gleaming metal of six hundred harnesses and six
hundred sabres. The Light Brigade positively
sparkled into action as the pace of the charge
quickened into a gallop. Sam began to catch the
excitement, the exhilaration of the battle and he
felt proud of the British cavalry. After all, hadn't
the Heavy Brigade defeated a very much larger
Russian force?

Then his thoughts were interrupted by a flood
of smoke and flame bursting forth from the
captured redoubts and from other parts of the
enemy lines. His mouth gaped open and he stared
wide-eyed for a moment as he finally saw for
himself what was happening. Joe had said
something was wrong. Whether it was Cardigan's
fault or someone else's, the Light Brigade was
charging directly at the enemy guns. The next
instant, Sam's feeling of pride and exultation were
shattered as a terrible thought flashed through
his mind. What if his father were wounded, or

much worse, killed?

Now the men were yelling madly and waving their sabres as they rushed headlong towards the Russian lines. Some were standing in their stirrups and all along the lines was the sound of frightened horses neighing. The boy heard the hiss of cannon balls, then the first line of riders was cut down, leaving men and horses lying all over the ground. Riderless mounts galloped off in all directions but still the charge continued. One wounded animal was left screaming and threshing on the ground. He searched anxiously among the soldiers on the left flank and saw his father still pressing forward, unaffected by the carnage all around.

The first riders reached the guns and Sam saw the sabres rising and falling as the brave cavalrymen cut down the enemy. Some of the gunners abandoned their positions and ran from the slaughter. Then, just as the guns were secured, Russians on the hillside opened fire, killing yet more of the already depleted cavalry. The shattered remains of the Light Brigade then began to return back up the valley and Sam stood up, waving his cap and cheering, while Joe vainly tried to drag him down again.

Then to Sam's horror an enormous detachment of Russian lancers galloped forward and tried to stop the British cavalry by charging into their flank. The Light Brigade fought back and some of the Russian gunners returned to their positions. They started firing directly into the struggling mass of soldiers, killing their own men and British alike. It was only then that the remnants of the heroic Light Brigade managed to struggle back to their own lines.

The headstrong Sam forgot the need for concealment and along with a host of fellow Britons ran out to meet them. The boy noticed, in a curiously detached way, that contrary to what he'd imagined some riders were totally uninjured. Others had slight flesh wounds while a number of the badly wounded got back only because they hadn't fallen off their horses. Although he'd noticed all this Sam had eyes for only one man and not the Brigade as a whole, and he searched anxiously among those returning. After the atrocity he had just witnessed he feared the worst and felt sick to the pit of his stomach. Moreover, recognition was difficult, as most of the survivors were dirty and dishevelled and many had bloody head wounds. In desperation he was compelled to walk up to passing riders and peer closely at them. One badly wounded sergeant with a shattered leg looked at the boy and cursed as an ambulance driver helped him from his horse.

It's no use, mused Sam in despair; the final cannonade must have finished him off. He was without a father for the second time in his life and his mother could never hope to support the family on her own. They'd be begging on the streets of London. He turned away, barely holding back the tears when he noticed a lone horseman, a good hundred yards behind the final stragglers, riding slowly along and swaying from side to side. It was his father. Good old Dad, thought Sam, trust him to be the last to retreat.

'Papa, it's me,' Sam called. Sam, the former street boy always thought of his father as Dad but now followed the middle-class practice of using Papa. As soon as he had spoken the dam burst and he gave vent to his passions. He wept great tears of relief, his shoulders shaking with sobs he tried to control but couldn't. A fatherly hand was placed on his head.

'Sam, what the heck are you doing here? I thought I told you to stay at home and look after your mother.' Puzzlement showed on Colonel Hopwood's face for a moment, then his eyes glazed and he slid slowly sideways from his saddle.

Sam glanced down and saw what he hadn't noticed before, the spreading claret stain discolouring the blue of the jacket sleeve. The feeling of despair returned more strongly than ever and he desperately wanted to cry again. But he made a tremendous effort and managed to control the tears. After all if he was to be of use to his father he had to remain calm. There was no point in being an ambulance man and collapsing in panic at the first sign of trouble.

His thoughts were interrupted as a soft tongue moistened his ear and a harsh sound cut through the thunder of the guns. 'Eeyore, eeyore,' went the voice and in the midst of conflict, the boy was comforted. His furry companion and friend had finally decided the time for pigheadedness was over and the time for action had arrived. Carrots was here to do his duty and wasn't going to be put off by a few guns. Then over the din of battle came the distant sound of one man shouting.

'Carrots back here this instant, back here I say,' yelled the frantic Joe as he hobbled down the hill towards them. Joe summed up the situation in an instant and forgot his difficulties with Carrots. 'Dad don't look too good, does he Sam? There's only one thing for it, we'll have to get him to the hospital at Balaclava, right away.'

'I think Carrots realised that before we did, that's why he came over. Normally he's as stubborn as a mule,' said the boy. That remark finally tipped Carrots over the edge and it took valuable minutes to pacify him. 'Sorry boy,' said Sam at last, 'I didn't mean to call you a mule.' Then they eased Colonel Hopwood up onto the cart.

Sam glanced around the battlefield taking in

the dead and the wounded as he did so. Somehow the charge didn't seem so glorious now. Some of the dead might be fathers too and now their children were without a father; wives were without a husband. For a moment he stood in silent prayer, remembering those who had fallen and praying for the recovery of the wounded.

And so it was that a mere five hours after they left, Sam and Joe made the dangerous return journey to the Church of Kadikoi. The little donkey with one shrivelled ear seemed quite unafraid of the noise and smoke of the battle. On one occasion, a lone Russian jumped in their path, aiming his musket at Sam. Carrots didn't hesitate for a moment and baring his teeth he charged straight at the man, who saved his life only by hurling himself into a ditch.

When they arrived, the primitive military hospital was already crowded with casualties from the Battle of Balaclava and it was only because Joe knew one of the surgeons that they managed to get the Colonel a bed. The two ambulance men then returned to the battle and their job of taking the wounded to the military hospitals. Afterwards Sam reflected that an evening spent working with real casualties under Joe's tuition was worth weeks of normal training. In fact he never did receive any formal teaching for ambulance work because, from that time on, he was always busy with sick and injured people who urgently needed help. And he learnt his trade with a will; he needed all the skill he could muster to help save his father's life. Apart from Joe, his only school was the one of experience and hard knocks.

It wasn't until the small hours of the morning that they returned to Balaclava, where they found Colonel Hopwood had developed a fever. An anxious Sam decided to sleep on the floor by his father's bed although, in truth, he slept little. Worry and the cries of the wounded kept him awake most of the night.

The next morning a medical orderly told Sam and Joe the Russians had been forced to retreat leaving the field in possession of the Allies. 'It was a near run thing at times. First thing this morning, the Russian cavalry nearly took Balaclava. It was only a small group of Highlanders under Sir Colin Campbell that stopped them. Of course he had some of the Turks who ran away from the redoubts but it was mainly the Scots that did it. The "thin red line" they're calling them.'

Over the next few days, Colonel Hopwood's condition worsened and it became obvious that the wound in his arm was infected. Much of the time he was in a shallow sleep in which he moaned softly to himself at the pain in his arm. It was at this time that Sam first realised the medical care provided for the Crimean soldiers was of a low standard. Most of the men died, not from their wounds but from diseases such as cholera and dysentery. The hospital was filthy, overrun with rats and a breeding ground for germs. There were few blankets and many soldiers had no option but to lie on beds dressed only in dirty blood-stained shirts. Nearly all had lice. There was much grumbling among the men, with commanders like Cardigan and Raglan being blamed for all the misery. Sam prayed almost continuously for the life of his father but he didn't forget the other poor wretches forced to lie among all the misery. However, it soon became obvious that his father would die in such surroundings unless something were done quickly. Sam remembered that Jesus had once applied ointment to the eyes of a blind woman before praying. Sometimes prayer alone was not enough.

The bloody Battle of Inkerman was fought less than two weeks after Balaclava. The Russians attacked from Inkerman, a ruined village just over a mile from Sebastopol and some six miles from Balaclava. This time there was little use for cavalry and the day consisted largely of vicious hand-to-hand combat between two sets of infantry. Eventually the second attempt to drive the Allies into the sea was defeated with heavy Russian losses and the enemy was forced to retreat and lick their wounds. There was a feeling among the Allies that this time they would not be back and it was just a matter of time before Sebastopol fell. But casualties were high among the Allies too, and the hospitals were so full that the doctors could not cope.

There was a large hospital at Scutari, near to Constantinople, over three hundred miles away on the other side of the Black Sea. But the wounded had to be transported by ship and many died on the way. There were also rumours that conditions there were as bad as in the Balaclava hospitals.

Colonel Hopwood was now delirious most of the time and often failed to recognise Sam even when fully conscious. The boy spoke with the army surgeon who was tending his father and the man's opinion as to his chances was not reassuring. 'I'm sorry to say he has a fever caused by the wound turning septic. I've seen so many of these cases in the past few weeks and I'm afraid I'm not optimistic. I'd say two or three weeks at the outside,' sighed the sad-faced doctor. Sam was devastated and the bitter tears flowed down his cheeks as he lay curled up on the floor next to his father's bed throughout the long watches of the night. It seemed that hope was gone and all he could do was sit it out till Colonel Hopwood died of his wounds. His newfound healing skills had proved useless.

It was there that the orderly found him in the morning and he listened gravely as the boy recounted his story. 'Actually, if you can get him across to Scutari, he might stand a chance. I've been hearing stories about a new woman they've put in charge of the nurses there and she's started cleaning things up. Her name's Nightingale, Florence Nightingale,' said the man. 'I'd do it if I were you. It's his only chance.'

Chapter 4

Florence Nightingale

The next morning Sam and Joe carefully placed Colonel Hopwood on a stretcher and took him by donkey cart down to the sick wharf at Balaclava harbour. This was the place where the sick and wounded were placed into rowing boats and ferried out to the hospital ship ready for transportation to Scutari. Joe was to stay behind on the ambulances while Sam and Carrots accompanied the Colonel to the hospital.

Conditions on board were as bad as, if not worse than the military hospitals, with many patients left on deck exposed to the elements while others were crammed together down below in squalid, suffocating conditions. Even the leaky hold where Carrots was kept was cleaner and healthier. Sam now had enough experience in the ways of medicine to know with an awful certainty that many would never get to Scutari alive. Worse, he now felt that his own father wouldn't make it.

The wound was now beginning to smell and the Colonel was in a kind of coma from which he occasionally wakened to babble nonsense about the charge of the Light Brigade. The boy ate and drank little during the week-long journey across the Black Sea but spent the time dozing fitfully in an old armchair in the corner of the cabin. His misery was increased by the rough weather, which made him feel queasy, and even Carrots seemed low.

The ship docked in Constantinople and Sam felt his spirits lift at his first sight of the hospital from across the Bosphorus, the narrow stretch of water that separated the city from Scutari. The imposing yellow building, with its four tall towers, looming out of the morning mist, looked to the desperate boy like the great palace of a sultan. Let's hope the treatment is as good as the building, thought Sam.

'Excuse me, but I've got sick men lying in the open outside the main gate. What do I have do to get them admitted?' shouted Sam as he tried to attract an orderly's attention. The boy had been in the hospital for at least half an hour and had achieved nothing. People were scurrying to and fro in all directions but there seemed to be no organisation and everyone was too busy to talk. The orderly looked harassed as he struggled to weave through the throng with a trolley-load of blankets.

'Sorry mate, nothing to do with me. You'll have to find a doctor.' The man nodded in the direction of a nearby door and then shuffled on his way.

The ward was no different from any he had seen in the Crimea, with wounded soldiers lying in filthy, overcrowded conditions on straw mattresses. Mostly the mattresses were on beds but many had been placed higgledy-piggledy close together on the floor so Sam was forced to step over them as he searched for a doctor. One young man was lying with an unbandaged wound exposed to the air and as the boy moved gingerly past, he noticed the large, jagged cut was gaping open and crawling with maggots. In his few years Sam had seen much suffering, both in London and the Crimea but even he retched and was forced to press his handkerchief to his lips to avoid throwing up his meagre breakfast.

At the far end of the ward, a group of men and women surrounded a bed where someone was screaming. This was not unusual in military hospitals and as the boy came closer he guessed that a surgeon had just finished amputating a leg. It was the kind of thing he had become all too expert at noticing. Now he could detect the smell of rum, often given to help reduce the pain of an operation and there was a blood-stained surgical saw resting on top of a medical bag. He reached the group and was about to ask about admission for the wounded when a young woman burst into the ward and strode purposefully towards them.

'Doctor Forester, you have been operating on that poor man without the use of chloroform. Don't bother to deny it, I can tell. Are you quite incapable of imagining how it must feel with nothing to deaden the pain?' she yelled at the surgeon. The doctor was a short fat man, bald apart from wispy white hair to the sides and back of his head, and as if to compensate, he had bushy side-whiskers. Sam guessed him to be in his early sixties.

'Chloroform! Can't bear the stuff. I much

prefer the swift use of a saw or even a knife. It's painful to be sure but it's better to hear a man bawl his lungs out than sink silently into the grave. I don't do anything to anyone else that I wouldn't have done to myself. I was with Wellington at Waterloo and got a musket ball in the knee, so I know what it's like, believe me.' The army surgeon wiped his hands on his blood-stained apron and hobbled awkwardly out from behind the bed. Sam glanced down at the wooden leg. Then the old soldier swabbed the blood from his saw, picked up his bag of instruments and walked away, the retinue of doctors and nurses in close attendance. 'Good-day to you Miss Nightingale, I've got work to do.'

'Good-day Dr Forester,' Florence Nightingale sighed. She looked at Sam in despair. 'He's a good man in his way but he's of the old school and he won't use anaesthetic. He's not concerned about hygiene either, and I'm sure that kills some of the patients.' So this is the nurse I've heard so much about, thought Sam. She was surprisingly young and pretty with her brown hair parted in the middle and held in place by a white lace cap. Her black gown, which was long enough to brush the floor, was topped by a starched white collar.

'What's anaesthetic, Florence?' said Sam nervously.

'Miss Nightingale to you my boy and don't you

forget it. Anaesthetic is a substance, such as chloroform, which deadens pain and sends you to sleep so that operations aren't painful. By the way, who are you, and pray, what are you doing wandering around the hospital?'

'I'm with the Hospital Conveyance Corps in Kadikoi and I came across the Black Sea with some wounded soldiers. They're lying outside now. But I've been here in the hospital for quite a while and it seems there's no one interested in admitting them,' said Sam. Miss Nightingale sighed.

'Come with me, boy. I can't keep calling you boy. What is your name?' she smiled.

'Sam, Miss Nightingale,' and he followed her back towards the entrance.

'As you can see, the place is a mess, absolutely filthy with no proper organisation and I'm sorry there was nobody available to meet your party. There are going to be changes around here I can assure you.' Her voice was firm, her eyes glinted and her jaw jutted as she spoke. Sam could see she meant what she said and felt comforted. 'God has sent me here to do a job and, by heaven, I'll do it,' she continued. 'The kingdom of heaven is within but we must also aim to bring it out into the wards of this hospital.'

By now they had reached the entrance and Miss Nightingale proceeded to examine the wounded. 'And who's this unconscious man here?' she said, kneeling down to examine him.

'That's my father, Colonel Hopwood, Miss Nightingale,' said the boy. 'He was wounded at Balaclava and I'm very worried about him. What do you think of his chances?'

Florence Nightingale looked grim and spoke softly, so only Sam could hear. 'I don't like to say this but I think you'll have to prepare for the worst. I'm very much afraid Colonel Hopwood isn't long for this world.' Sam bit his lip savagely and fought back the tears. He had to remain strong at all costs.

'Excuse me Sergeant, I wonder if you can help me,' she said to an off-duty redcoat lounging against the wall. 'Could you possibly arrange a detachment of your guards to get these patients into a ward?' Miss Nightingale smiled charmingly at the soldier.

'Certainly ma'am, right away,' said the man as he hurried off to find his men.

She turned back to Sam. 'You see how I'm fixed. I have to be a diplomat. I have no control over soldiers; I'm just the Lady Superintendent in charge of nurses.'

Sam spoke with a quiet desperation. 'Are you absolutely certain you can do nothing for the Colonel?' he blurted. 'I've been working on the ambulances back in the Crimea and I've seen lots of men die. I thought I could do something for my papa, though. They said that if I brought him here he had a chance.'

Florence Nightingale opened her mouth to speak and then stopped and knitted her brow. 'Well there is young Dr Galton, who finished training at St Bartholemew's in London last year. I'll ask him if he can do anything. He works in the part of the hospital I've had cleaned up.'

'The chloroform is placed in the bottle then the mouthpiece is placed right over the patient's nose and mouth. So, when he breathes in, he gets a mixture of air and chloroform. Then Bob's your uncle, it all comes right, before you know it he's out like a light.' Young Dr Galton rolled his eyes then buckled his legs in imitation of unconsciousness, and despite himself Sam laughed. 'Of course we don't have many of these bottles in Scutari. What we normally do is soak a handkerchief in chloroform and place it over the face. And some of the surgeons won't even do that, as no doubt Florence has told you.' Dr Galton was a genial fellow who was explaining to Sam the latest medical advance to come out of London.

The boy glanced around the ward with its neat rows of beds and air of cleanliness and efficiency. Soon the whole hospital would be like this if Florence Nightingale had her way.

'I've had to cut most of Colonel Hopwood's

shirt sleeve away and once he's had a shot of chloroform I can start. I don't promise I can save him, mind,' continued the doctor. Now go and sit down somewhere so I've got some elbow room. Sam did as he was asked but kept a careful eye on proceedings. He was beginning to feel that his future would be in medicine. He didn't know how it would come about or what exactly he would be doing but he somehow just knew that God wanted him to work in healing. His ambulance work was for a purpose.

The first thing he noticed was that the doctor's surgical instruments were all spotlessly clean and they were used with great skill. It was the early hours of the morning when a dozing Sam felt a hand on his shoulder. 'I've done all I can, the pus is drained out of the wound and now only time will tell. If he's a fighter he'll probably make it. If not, well....'

Sam felt oddly reassured by the young man's manner and he knew his father was a fighter, so there was still hope. When he finally dropped off into a slumber his mood was one of confidence in the future, something he had not experienced for weeks.

It was three days before Colonel Hopwood regained consciousness. Florence Nightingale had wisely kept Sam busy helping clean up the hospital to stop him dwelling on his father's fate.

The boy was on the worst job of all, visiting each of the four towers in turn and cleaning out the privies, when Dr Galton found him.

'It's your father, he's awake and wants to speak with you.' Sam threw his scrubbing brush into the air and ran whooping with joy to the ward. The Colonel was smiling and waiting, sitting in bed propped up by pillows when the boy blew in like a whirlwind and threw his arms around his neck. Naturally he selected the uninjured side and then stayed there hugging him furiously for a good ten minutes. Finally, a laughing Colonel Hopwood pulled himself free and gave Sam a kiss.

'As you can see old chap, I'm still in the land of the living but I need to give you a piece of my mind. I'm not pleased with you for running away from your mother and I won't pretend I am. Have you written to her yet? She must be worried sick.'

Sam hung his head in shame and went red in the face but said nothing. 'I can see by the look of you that you haven't and you should be ashamed of yourself,' the Colonel continued. 'I want you to sit down and write her a letter today. Do you promise?'

'I promise, Papa,' sobbed the boy. Then the dam broke and he burst into such tears of guilt and shame that it took all his father's patient coaxing to calm him down.

'There, there son,' he said at length. 'Dr Galton

and Miss Nightingale have been telling me of your courage in getting me here. Then you had to move heaven and earth to obtain the right treatment. I'll allow you to stay with me until such time as I go home, how's that? Now be off with you and write your letter. And by the way, happy birthday.'

'Thank you Papa,' shouted Sam, and off he trotted to write to his mother. How silly of me thought Sam as he sat there pen in hand. Two days ago it was my fourteenth birthday and in all that was going on I quite forgot. As he sat there the boy poured all his emotions into writing the letter, telling his mother why he followed his father and how he was sorry that he had deceived her and that he hoped she was well. He also asked after his sister Sophie, born in 1852, the year after the Hopwoods adopted him. She was two years old now and he realised how he missed her. He broke off and wept bitterly for several minutes before continuing.

The boy went on to relate how his father was wounded, and how he, Sam, a trainee ambulance man, had got him to hospital in the Crimea and then in Scutari. He told her about Florence Nightingale and Dr Galton and how he now knew that God wanted him to work in medicine. The letter finished by saying how Colonel Hopwood was now on the road to recovery and that he hoped she would forgive him for all the wrong he had done.

Every day letters for home were collected from the hospital and put on the next ship to England. But Sam was too impatient for this so he took a trip across the Bosphorus with Carrots and gave the letter directly to the boatswain of a steamer bound for Southampton that very day. With luck he would get a reply by Christmas.

The days passed and the Colonel grew stronger thanks to the dedicated care of the nurses. It was Florence Nightingale's firm belief that the sick needed good food in order to recover. And she made sure they got it. She also criticised the army for not feeding its soldiers properly; **The Times** published her comments and the politicians in London had to take notice. From that time on the military diet started to improve.

Sam was put to work cleaning up the hospital. He had already scoured the privies and now they had to be kept spotless. Along with other volunteers and staff he scrubbed window frames, floors and walls in those parts of the building (most of it) that still needed bringing up to Florence Nightingale's standards. It was hard work too. The ceilings were supported by strong stone arches where crevices held dirt and the gaps in the flagstones on the floor provided a gathering place for rubbish. The central yard, littered with refuse that attracted vermin, took several days of backbreaking work to clear.

From time to time shiploads of beds, tables, chairs and kitchen equipment arrived from Britain and these had to be carried up to the rooms. These items came largely as the result of a campaign by influential people, such as John Thadeus Delane, editor of *The Times*.

Gradually, as conditions improved, even the smell of the hospital changed. At one time there had been a stench of mingled sweat, dirt, dust and rubbish. And in the background, the all-pervading odour of blocked privies. Then one day Sam stood in the main corridor, sniffed the air and detected only carbolic soap and chloroform.

Florence Nightingale would visit on her rounds most evenings, carrying her lamp to help her through dimly-lit wards and corridors. She was greatly admired by the troops, who called her 'the lady with the lamp'.

Although she was personally friendly to a degree, she was always reserved and Sam thought this might be because of the strain of getting things done in the teeth of so much opposition. His impression was confirmed when once he passed her quarters in the small hours of the morning. The door was ajar and she was kneeling at her prayers. Firstly she prayed for many of the patients by name, including Colonel Hopwood. Then she prayed for her nurses to be firm and gentle in their work, just like Jesus, and for the doctors that they would put the needs of the patients first. She continued with a special prayer for those on the battlefront, including the Hospital Conveyance Corps and her young assistant Sam Hopwood. And finally she cried out in a loud voice, which seemed close to tears, for God to 'give me the strength to fulfill my responsibilities'.

Sam felt himself come out in goose bumps at being mentioned by name in her prayers and yet he thought that he respected her rather than liked her. When she was trying to influence important people from London she was all smiles and charm, yet she could also be arrogant and self-righteous. Once Sam overheard her talking to an officer: 'The soldiers have more respect for me than they do for you.'

Soon Colonel Hopwood was capable of standing up and he began to perform simple duties, such as feeding the badly wounded. As he recovered, Sam took him for rides on the donkey cart. Carrots was stabled in a wooden shed at the back of the hospital near to the cemetery. At first it was necessary for Sam to help his father through the hospital building to get to the stable but in time he could reach it unaided. The early trips involved just the town of Scutari, then came the countryside around it and finally, a few days before Christmas, they went on a sightseeing tour of Constantinople.

It was right after the tour that Colonel Hopwood received a letter from the army. 'I've to report back to Headquarters by the first of January. I'll be on light duties for the first two weeks and then I'll be assigned to escort duty. There's not much call for cavalry now we're besieging Sebastopol. Apparently I'll be in charge of a small troop escorting the army wages wagon, "the treasure wagon" the troops call it. You're to come with me and resume ambulance duty. You're certainly experienced enough in medical matters, now,' laughed his father.

On Christmas Eve, as Sam was helping decorate the hospital for the Christmas festivities, a letter arrived from his mother. In it she said that although she had been devastated at first when he had disappeared leaving only a short note, she had not only forgiven him but was proud of his work with the ambulances. She was also pleased about the way he had saved his father. 'Perhaps it was God at work telling you to go to the Crimea,' she said.

Sam felt good after reading the letter and felt he had been pardoned for his wrongs. Enclosed in the envelope was a recent sepia photograph of Sophie and his mother, carefully posed in the photographer's shop in Poplar High Street, near his home. There was also a folded picture card with 'Merry Christmas' written on it. 'I've enclosed this novelty I bought in Oxford Street for you and your father, it's called a Christmas card. They're all the rage nowadays, so the assistant told me.' At the bottom his mother signed with her love to both of them and there was even a little cross drawn in crayon by Sophie.

That evening a choir, formed from the men of several regiments, visited the various wards to sing Christmas carols. The following day was Christmas Day and a Christmas dinner with a choice of turkey or goose was served to all the patients. Friends and relatives in Britain had sent boxes of seasonal foods such as puddings, cakes, mince pies, apples, oranges and nuts. Even Florence Nightingale was prevailed upon to drink an afternoon glass of sherry and the nurses became merry enough to dance with the soldiers. By the evening a general feeling of cheerfulness and good will pervaded the hospital. That night Sam went to bed content, confident in the knowledge that his life was again secure.

Chapter 5

Sebastopol

By mid-January, Colonel Hopwood and his cavalry detachment had escorted their first treasure wagon from Balaclava to British Headquarters and Sam went back to work with

Joe. He found the Hospital Conveyance Corps had been a complete disaster because many of the Chelsea Pensioners were simply too old to cope with the work. Some were heavy drinkers who were sent home to Britain, others had died of cholera, and the remainder was put under the direct command of regimental surgeons. Sam and Joe were detailed to serve the gunners of the Royal Artillery.

Usually the work consisted of conveying sick soldiers to hospital, but sometimes the Russian guns fired from behind the walls of Sebastopol and there were wounded to tend. One raw February day, Sam was bandaging a nasty gash in a corporal's leg when the boy became aware of a shadow in the room.

'Hey, English, how you? How your father?' Sam turned to see his gypsy friend, grinning as broadly as ever.

'Ishmael,' yelled Sam as he threw his arms round him. 'Good to see you. How are your parents?'

'Parents well, English, but treasure wagon is in danger. I come at daybreak tomorrow and show you.'

'Wait a minute Ishmael. Why is the treasure wagon in danger? In any case, how do you know about the treasure wagon?'

'We Romanies know many things, English. We

keep nose to ground, that way we stay safe. Russian bandits and British Army deserters, they get together. They want the treasure,' continued Ishmael. 'I show you early tomorrow morning,' and then, before Sam could stop him, he slid silently out of the hospital door.

Soon after daybreak on a bitter January day, Sam found himself crawling on hands and knees through the dense undergrowth perilously close to Fort Quarantine at the north-western end of the Sebastopol defensive wall. A heavy sleet borne on the north wind lashed his body and his fingers were numb with cold. Several times on their journey, Ishmael, who was without any sense of irony, had warned them to 'freeze' to avoid discovery by the sentries. There were three of them, including Mireli who was as skilled as her brother in the art of concealment.

The city wall loomed above in the twilight as Sam and Mireli each made a crouching run and followed Ishmael into a beach-side cave that dripped water and reeked of seaweed. Inside the damp enclosure the temperature seemed lower than ever. On the far side was a dense strip of bushes and then they were walking silently on city streets. They had achieved something no Allied soldier had since the beginning of the war—they'd entered the walled city of Sebastopol and what's more, they were free.

'English, come and meet my friend. He safe, he not give us away.' How could Ishmael think of visiting a friend now, of all times? Sam was in civilian clothes but if the little group were challenged he'd certainly be taken prisoner simply because he spoke no Russian.

They were now on a beach, deserted apart from themselves and one other who, despite the cold, sat at a wooden table, writing furiously. 'Leo, it's me Ishmael, meet my sister Mireli and my friend Sam.' At least that's what Sam thought Ishmael was saying, because he actually spoke in Russian. Leo was an interesting-looking man, in his twenties, Sam guessed, with brown straggly hair. His nose was broad and he was bearded, with a ready smile that twinkled from his eyes. The uniform was familiar to the English boy; Ishmael's friend was an officer of the Russian Artillery.

Firstly he shook hands with the Romany children, laughing and joking in Russian, and then he turned to Sam. 'And how did you get to know Ishmael?' asked Leo in clear but heavily accented English.

Sam was so surprised he was dumbstruck at first and felt his face turn red. Then he tried to answer but only got as far as 'Balaclava'.

'Don't worry Sam, I could tell at once you're not a gypsy and Ishmael once told me about an

English friend of his. Ishmael's in and out of Sebastopol the whole time, you know. He's as slippery as an eel. Anyway, I won't tell my army friends that you're here.'

'What are you writing about?' stammered Sam at length.

'I write all the time; it's my life. I write about anything and everything,' said the Russian suddenly becoming animated. 'I am a Christian, a follower of Christ and I want to bring his message to a world hungry for his word. It is my ambition to write novels that are full of Christian morals. I am a man of peace, you understand, but here I sit in a soldiers's uniform and that is very strange, I think you'll agree. That's the kind of problem I want to write about.' He was totally engrossed in his subject, like an actor in a play, using his hands, grey eyes flashing.

'I'm a Christian and I work taking wounded men to hospital. And my father he's also a Christian. He was wounded when his cavalry brigade charged right into your guns,' Sam cut in excitedly.

'Ah, yes, the Light Brigade, all that valour! Such misplaced bravery, I admire those men greatly. But what a pity that two Christian men, your father and myself, should be trying to kill each other. This should never be.' Leo suddenly looked sad.

'Do people read what you write?' asked Sam,

suddenly feeling uncomfortable about the Russian's words.

'Not many but soon they will,' Leo smiled. 'One day I'll be world famous, like your own Charles Dickens. Mr Pickwick, Oliver Twist, Old Scrooge,' he chuckled.

'English, we need to go, the meeting will start.' It was Ishmael, calling him away.

Leo leaned forward and shook Sam's hand. 'Count Leo Tolstoy at your service, goodbye and God speed.'

The way from the beach led through a small wood. At the far end was a low stone wall, which the three children vaulted in turn. 'We're nearly there English, the church I told you about.'

Sam followed Ishmael and Mireli as the two gypsies moved expertly through the churchyard. They seemed so calm, so self-assured, Sam thought yet he could feel his own heart pounding furiously and he was glad of the chance to catch his breath crouching behind a large crumbling tomb. Here Ishmael took the opportunity to look behind for possible pursuers and then, satisfied, he sat down on the damp grass and grinned. The young gypsy was completely relaxed, a boy without a care in the world, and Mireli was just as calm.

Why are they so confident? Sam mused as he hunched down into his army greatcoat and shivered at the misty gravestones. Probably because they'd been hunted all their lives and take it for granted, he concluded. Despite the Allied bombardment the stone tablets were quite undamaged, although there was a shell crater not ten yards from the children and the outer wall had been breached, allowing vegetation from the woods beyond to spill through. The boy could hear the twittering of bird song and smell the sweet dampness of the pine trees.

'English, it is time to go.' Sam jerked out of his reverie and stood up, then they ran, half crouching, to the stone wall of the church building. He found himself standing on a rubble of old bricks filling what had obviously been a small ditch or narrow moat. Ishmael flung his arms around a small bush and dragged it to one side.

'See, there.' Sam looked and noticed a hole among the bricks about big enough for a man to wriggle through. Ishmael was right; it was not something people would know about. ' It was put there by a priest the Tsar hated, so they say. When the soldiers came he'd escape through the hole.'

Now the gypsy boy was scrabbling around in the rubble and Sam saw a wooden cover with a heavy metal ring at one end gradually being exposed to view. 'English, help me, this door is, how you say, heavy?' Sam lay by the edge of the hole and the two boys took a firm grasp of the ring, but it was only after several minutes of straining that the cover moved and then only slightly. That was enough and Ishmael carefully pushed a brick underneath. They rested, panting and sweating for a few minutes, then wrestled the heavy object to one side, exposing a flight of steps leading down into the darkness.

The gypsy gave a broad grin. 'I go first, eh English,' and he eased himself into the opening. Sam saw the shock of curly hair fast disappearing into the blackness below, Mireli followed and then he went after them.

By the light of the opening above Sam could see the two Romanies half standing in front of a low passageway that could have been an old drain. Ishmael and Mireli dropped to their knees and started to crawl at high speed while the larger Sam followed, stumbling and clumsily scuffing his back as he went. Pausing to catch his breath, Sam could no longer hear his companions and realised they had arrived at the end. 'We're inside, under the floor,' said Ishmael when Sam caught up, dishevelled and sweating. The chinks between the boards provided just enough light for them to see. 'Over there English, there's a gap near the stairs.'

Within seconds they were sitting at the bottom of a flight of stairs, their feet dangling into the hole in the floor from which they came. Sam stood up to take his bearings and carefully examined the interior of the church. All the great, stained-glass windows were broken and the weak winter sunlight was streaming in. There were pale, rectangular marks all over the walls and the shapes told Sam pictures had hung there. He remembered his father telling him that Russian churches were famous for their beautiful paintings. They were called Ikons and they all had themes from the Bible. Since the siege began the poor people of Sebastopol had suffered greatly and the boy guessed that the pictures had been stolen by the locals to buy food. There were always rich merchants prepared to pay good money for works of art to decorate the halls and lounges of their country houses. And not ask too many questions.

To the left of the stairs was a large area leading to the front of the church. Sam guessed this was where the altar was located. He was about to walk round and investigate when he heard the murmur of voices. The boy froze to the spot and then frantically motioned the children to climb the stairs. They bounded to their feet and glided swiftly and soundlessly up the staircase. Sam kept close behind as the steps wound to the left and they soon found themselves in a rickety loft space high above the altar.

The room was full of junk, mainly boxes and broken furniture. It was very dusty and large cobwebs hung from the ceiling. The only light came from places where tiles were missing from the roof. 'Over here English,' said Ishmael in a stage whisper. In one corner part of a board had been sawn away, giving a perfect view of what lay below. 'They can't see us, it's very dark above the altar,' continued the gypsy. 'I know because I've been down there and looked up.'

The three children lay face down in the dust peering closely at the scene beneath them. Sam could see a table with perhaps a dozen men seated on boxes. On one side was a group dressed roughly in the Russian peasant style, where a powerfully built man with black hair and a bushy beard appeared to stand out.

'Who's that?' asked Sam quietly.

'That's Ivan, the leader of the Crimean bandits. He bribes a Russian general to let him use this place. That way he is safe from both the Allies and the Russians. Look at their weapons, the two groups don't trust each other,' replied Ishmael.

In front of Ivan, on the table top, was a long knife with a curved blade, and he wore a pistol in his belt. The rest of his gang were little different except that the guns and daggers varied in style. One was picking his teeth with a stiletto while another casually cleaned his blunderbuss. At least two of the men carried swords.

The deserters were in the half shadow of the other side of the table so weapons were only hinted at by the occasional glint of steel in the darkness.

Ivan spoke for a few minutes, pausing from time to time to allow an interpreter to translate.

Then a voice started speaking in English, a voice that seemed oddly familiar yet Sam couldn't quite place it. But it made him uneasy. His eyes were now more used to the darkness and he saw uniforms, mainly British with at least one French and one Turkish, belonging to the deserters.

'So tomorrow afternoon it is then, three o'clock at this place you speak of near Kadikoi.' The man leaned forward into a patch of sunlight shining in from a hidden window. Sam just lay and stared in horror, then nearly cried out, stopping himself only with a great effort of will. The man below, the leader of the deserters, was Razor George.

'English, what's wrong? You seen a ghost?' His friend looked anxious.

'The man with the shaven head, I know him. He came over on the same ship as me and he hates me. We need to get back and tell my father. I don't want him wounded again,' whispered Sam frantically.

'We go English,' said Ishmael. He turned and whistled softly to Mireli who had become bored and was balancing on top of an old cupboard. The girl raised her hand in answer but as she jumped her foot tipped the flimsy structure backwards making it crash to the floor. The group below scattered like a flock of starlings frightened by the noise of a gun and a frantic scrum formed round the church door. Terrified bandits swore and fought with each other in an effort to get out first.

Ishmael ran to the top of the stairs beckoning the others to follow.

'Wait a moment, we'll let them clear the door and then go. We should have a few minutes to escape before they dare show their faces here again,' said Sam, forcing himself to remain calm despite the desperate situation. As soon as the church was empty the three children ran silently into the churchyard and jumped the wall at the back.

Under Ishmael's sure guidance they were soon back at Fort Quarantine. Sam knew they might be followed and had kept watch during their flight but saw nobody. By the time he reached Carrots, tethered to a tree about a mile outside the city wall, he felt secure. Soon he would be with his father and tomorrow's attack would probably at least be put off, mused Sam.

The children jumped up onto the cart and Sam had just started to drive away when he felt a pressure at the side of his neck. Slowly he turned his head to see Razor George squatting by his side, pistol in hand.

'Keep goin' you little varmint, only you ain't goin' back to no camp, you're comin' with me. And you'll be sorry you got on the wrong side of Razor George, I can tell yer.' Sam couldn't turn round but he heard Mireli scream and then two soft thuds as the two gypsies jumped from the cart. He knew Razor George would never catch them. In any case he was too busy with Sam. Within an hour they would raise the alarm, except that no one knew where he was being taken.

Under Razor George's directions he drove up into the hills, following the course of a river, which Sam guessed was probably the Chernaya, as the Alma was further away and to the north of Sebastopol. Then just before sunset they arrived at a tumbledown farmhouse half hidden behind trees. Ivan and a group of bandits stood by a wooden gate awaiting their arrival.

'Get down and unhitch the donkey,' snarled George. Sam did as he was told and Carrots was soon free of his cart. He looked up to see Ivan bearing down on him, a great fist swinging for his head. Sam ducked but failed to fully evade the blow and the force of it sent him sprawling in the grass. What would have happened next he could only guess. Perhaps Ivan intended to kill him but he never had the chance to find out. Carrots moved like lightening to arch his back and distribute his weight onto his forelegs. Then before the Russian could move,the hind legs, tipped with iron hooves, smashed into his chest. The man shot backwards like a rocket, his shoulder blades striking the gate with crunching force before falling, gasping and twitching to the ground.

'Come on you little rat, see how you like the inside of the barn.' George grabbed Sam by the collar and frog-marched him to a long wooden building while the others tended Ivan. As he was shoved inside, Sam saw Carrots being taken to the stables opposite, braying in triumph. The boy couldn't resist smiling when he saw the nervous way the men handled him, prodding him with long poles and keeping well out of reach of his hind legs.

Sam sat down on a bale of straw and thought miserably of the mess he was in. His father was in danger and he, Sam, could do nothing and what was more his own life was in peril. George might be back to finish him off at any minute. He stood up and frantically searched the barn for ways of escape but there was none. The one window was tightly barred and in any case there was a guard outside. Then he remembered something his father had told him.

'I've been a soldier a few years now and I've been in a tight corner or two, I can tell you. And one thing I've learnt is that God is always with you on these occasions and you sense his presence much more clearly than in your workaday life. Always pray if ever you find yourself in a fix and he won't let you down.'

Sam dropped to his knees and thanked God for

all that he had done and than asked him to find a way of helping his father. Then he lay down, covered himself in an old sack to keep warm and finally dozed out of sheer exhaustion. It must have been late at night that he heard noises in the yard. He rushed to the window to see the yard filled with horses and men. Ivan, his open shirt revealing tight strapping on his chest was being helped on his mount by two Russians. He sat slumped over the animal's neck, obviously in great pain and then, only with a great effort, motioned the gang to move out. George looked up at the window and shook his fist. 'We'll deal with you tomorrow.' Despite everything it looks like the attack is going ahead, thought Sam. They probably think our soldiers won't listen to two gypsy children and sadly, they're right.

Sam was still at the window half an hour later when he heard distant whistling from outside. It sounded like some kind of signal but he couldn't be sure. Somewhere out in the darkness he thought he saw horsemen. But why should Ivan's men be signalling, wondered Sam? He looked down at the yard and his heart leapt when he saw Ishmael standing in the shadows. He shouted and the gypsy looked up.

'Wait there English, we get you out.' He pushed his finger and thumb between his lips and whistled. Within minutes two gypsy riders appeared. One of them smashed the lock with a hammer and Sam was free. 'We Romanies know this place. The bandits from here always attack us and steal our horses,' said Ishmael by way of explanation. 'Boat in River Chernaya, near tree across water. Carrots is free, you escape and warn your father. I go now, if bandits come back they kill gypsies.' And then he was gone like a will o' the wisp into the darkness. The door of the stable banged open in the wind and there stood Carrots looking pleased with himself. There was no sign of the cart and time was short. He would just have to leave it behind.

Chapter 6

Mary Seacole

Sam looked round for Ishmael but the gypsy boy and his companions had slipped away like shadows. He was a hundred yards from the farmhouse now and there was no sign of the bandits either. He scoured the banks of the Chernaya looking for the boat. He was nervous, mindful of the barn that had so recently been his prison, but he forced himself to be strong and control his fear. The search wouldn't be easy, the bushy banks were overgrown and much of the river was choked with reeds. Carrots picked his way gingerly along the bank until Sam noticed a stunted tree leaning out across the water. This must be the spot Ishmael was trying to describe. And sure enough, there among the green of the reeds was a hint of brown. He shouted in triumph and eased the donkey down the steep embankment.

It was obviously not going to be a simple matter to manoeuvre Carrots into the boat. He estimated that the craft was about fifteen feet long and decided the donkey would have to go in the stern, otherwise his view would be restricted. Luckily the boat was fairly wide with a flat bottom but even so it took the best part of half an hour, in and out of icy water, to persuade the nervous donkey to stand on a floor that rocked beneath him. Just as well we're not being pursued, thought Sam. He knelt on the floor, breathed another prayer that he could manage a strange boat on a strange river, then gently lifted an oar and pushed it against the bank. As soon as the boat drifted into mid river, he positioned the oars carefully in the rowlocks and rowed quietly downstream. Everything was going smoothly. Once more God had answered his prayer.

The Chernaya was scarcely more than a stream up on the heights and what with the reeds and the water weed it was difficult to steer a way through. Several times he got stuck and was forced to step down into chilly sludge and push the bows back into clear water. Gradually the river widened and his rowing technique improved. By now he was moving quite fast and he noticed a strong forward current developing as the Chernaya took on a slight downward slope. As dawn broke he began to make out a frost-covered landscape. It was grassland with few trees and in the distance, far below, he could see the sea, together with Sebastopol and its harbour. He was even able to trace the course of the river with the old familiar Inkerman Bridge, near the battlefield where so many soldiers, from both sides, had died. Beyond the bridge, the Chernaya reached Inkerman Bay on the north side of Sebastopol.

Moving at speed and with no sign of the gang, Sam became confident, even cheerful and optimistic about getting to his father on time. He entered a valley shouting with joy and listened to the echo from the steep rocky walls as he journeyed on his way. The current became faster and the wind shrieked in his ears. Then came a roaring noise, barely audible at first over the wind but slowly it grew louder. He heard tumbling water and upon rounding a bend in the river he saw the cause. There were rocks submerged in the river and white foam frothed about them. He was approaching some rapids and the boat seemed to have a mind of its own. The current had become too fast for him and all he could do was hope for the best.

He avoided the first rock by fending it off with an oar but then completely lost control. The boat span wildly then hit a rock, and the world turned upside down. There was a roaring in his ears as the current bore him downwards till he found himself scraping along the gravel of the river bed. There was no escape, he was going to die, his lungs ached fit to burst and he just had to breathe. The next moment his head broke the surface and he inhaled greedily, his breath coming in great wheezing gasps. Carrot's head emerged from the water, then disappeared again as the surging current wrested control from his struggling form. Then Sam heard another sound, a deep thundering roar even more frightening than that of the rapids.

In a moment he was plunging downwards over a waterfall before meeting the foaming chaos below. Bits of debris from the boat bobbed all around him and he was sucked under again. He hit a rock and felt the blood flow. The current bore him up and he surfaced, moving at breakneck speed through the lower rapids. He knew he was done for if he hit just one rock at this pace. The surging stream pulled him near the bank like a bobbing cork and the overhanging branch of a tree, dangling near the surface, reared up in front of him. Seizing the opportunity he grasped the branch with both hands. The force nearly wrenched his arms from their sockets but he held on, losing skin from his palms in the process. Sam screamed in agony, then rallied for one final effort, twisting himself to one side with his remaining strength, before rolling exhausted onto the muddy bank.

He wasn't sure how long he lay there, racked with pain from his shoulders and hands, but finally he sat up when he remembered Carrots. He had last seen the donkey being sucked under just before the waterfall and the chances of a bulky animal surviving such a drop were small. He had to face facts, his faithful friend was dead and life without him would be unbearable. And if that wasn't bad enough, his father was in danger and there was now no way of warning him. Sam sat on the riverbank and felt devastated. He never knew how long he lay there, bitterly lamenting the fate that had overtaken him.

When, at last, he had finally done he got to his feet in a new mood of determination. I've been wasting valuable time in self-pity; after all, my father's fate rests in my hands, Sam thought. If only I can get my bearings, I might still be able to warn him.

He looked at the steep cliffs that flanked the river and decided to attempt the climb. At the top he hoped for a view of Sebastopol by which he could locate the British Army. The ascent wasn't that difficult, although his sore hands made it painful to grip the stunted bushes and trees that grew in the rocky crevices. The outdoor life of an ambulance driver had toughened him and he arrived at the top breathing almost normally. In a moment or two he'd located Sebastopol from the sound of cannon fire, then looked for signs of the Army. There were plenty of red coats in evidence close to the city wall and he prepared to run down to deliver his message.

He had just started when he heard a woman's voice from somewhere over his shoulder. 'Quite a view from here, boy.' Sam turned to see a middle-aged woman mounted on a mule. Considering the roughness of the terrain the clothes she wore were eccentric and certainly unsuitable. Her riding dress was very stylish, tartan in pattern and perched on her head was a large floppy hat with a feather. The colour of her skin, a pale brown, made her unusual to say the least, particularly on the battlefields of the Crimea. Working as a shoe black at the Great Exhibition and then living near the London docks, Sam had grown used to seeing people of colour from all parts of the world. But out here the unexpected sight must have made him stare, because the next thing he remembered was the sound of her voice.

'What's wrong with you, boy, standin' there with your mouth gapin' open. Ain't you never seen a Creole woman before?' She spoke with a lilt that Sam struggled hard to identify but failed.

'Well no I haven't, well I don't think I have. What's a Creole?' said Sam, at the same time feeling ashamed and a little confused.

'Mrs Mary Seacole of Kingston, Jamaica, at your service.' She shook Sam's hand with a vice-like grip that was as strong as a man's. 'Creole, well boy, you see my father was from Scotland and my mother was a woman of partly African descent. That's Creole. And I can't keep calling you boy. What's your name?'

'Sam Hopwood, Ma'am. My father's in the army and I've been working as an ambulance driver. At least I was before my donkey drowned in the Chernaya.' There was a catch in his voice as he thought of Carrots and he paused to stem the tears.

'No need to call me ma'am, Aunty Seacole will do. All the soldier boys call me that and a good few of the officers too.' She gave him a big smile, then laughed out loud. Her mood was so infectious that Sam found himself laughing despite his problems. 'This donkey you talk of, he's not a cussed, angry-looking creature with a shrivelled ear, by any chance? Only a soggy looking jackass covered in pond weed and wearing a collar came up to me about half an hour ago. He was nuzzlin' around in my bag and seemed hungry so I gave him some sugar lumps. I knew he must belong to somebody so I tethered him over there.' She gestured towards a tree not twenty yards away and there was Carrots contentedly munching the grass.

Sam ran across and flung his arms round the donkey's neck while Carrots made little contented grunting noises in his throat. When the reunion was over and the boy had regained his composure, he fished around in his pocket and produced a wrinkled carrot; all that was left after his enforced dip. The donkey swallowed it in one gulp, more to please Sam than for his own pleasure, then the normal look of vague annoyance returned to his face as the boy climbed on his back and steered him to Mary Seacole.

'Aunty Seacole, I've got to find my father as quickly as possible, his life is in danger,' said Sam in anxious tones. 'There's a gang of criminals made up of Crimean bandits and British deserters, plotting to ambush the treasure wagon. I've just escaped from their hideout upriver, that's how Carrots and me nearly got drowned. My father, Colonel Hopwood, is the officer of the guard escorting the wagon from the docks at Balaclava. The gang will be hiding at the top of the hill near Kadikoi, waiting for them when they come past at about three o'clock. We might be too late already.'

'You ain't having me on are you boy? Otherwise you and me are going to fall out.' Mary took one look at the miserable, bedraggled Sam and decided he was telling the truth. Then she pulled out a large fob watch from her top pocket. 'Twelve o'clock. We've still got time but we must hurry.'

'So you're going to help me?' said Sam sounding surprised. 'But I've only just met you so why should you bother?'

'Sam, there's a lot you don't know about me but I'll tell you one thing. I came half way across the world to be in this place, helping people,' said Mary. 'But we'll never get to Kadikoi if we don't get a move on and in any case you need a change of clothes.' So saying she tapped her mule on the rump and trotted off, leaving Sam to follow behind on Carrots. They had been facing west out towards the Black Sea and Mary Seacole now turned and headed south past the Inkerman battlefield onto a narrow track known as the Post Road.

'It's about eight miles to Kadikoi from here,'

shouted Mary as Sam drew level. 'I think it must be your lucky day because I run a hotel at Kadikoi, right by the Balaclava Road. It's called the British Hotel. When I say hotel, it's really a kind of combined general store and restaurant for the Army, although you get plenty of others, like French and Turks, comin' in,' she chuckled. 'I also keep my medicines there because I do nursin', helpin' the wounded soldier boys.'

'Do you think your hotel customers will be able to help me?' asked Sam anxiously.

'I certainly hope so,' said Mary. 'We've Major-General Sir John Campbell dropping in at about one. If he can't do anything, nobody can.'

Sam was pleased at this and his spirits began to rise. After all, he reasoned, a Major-General has influence and can get things done. By now they were sharing the road with a motley crowd of soldiers, mostly from Scottish and English regiments, and the boy began to recognise the land near the British Camp, not far from Kadikoi.

A few minutes later Mary turned off the road towards a large wooden shed situated hard by a fast-flowing brook. 'This place is Spring Hill,' shouted Mary over her shoulder, 'and the buildin' is my hotel.' She jumped down with an agility remarkable for a woman of mature years, tethered her mule to a wooden rail and strode through the high wooden doorway. Sam would have followed straight away but somehow the sight of a mule tied up and unable to move brought out Carrot's worst tendencies and he proceeded to butt the unfortunate animal unmercifully. Only with great difficulty was he dragged off and bound to another rail, with Sam desperately shouting commands like 'whoa there', 'naughty' and 'bad boy'. But it was no use; Carrots had an unrelenting air of being pleased with himself that his master knew only too well. With the donkey in one of his smug moods there was only one thing for it and that was to walk away.

The inside of the hotel looked like a large general store stacked from top to bottom with tins, jars and bottles of every description. The variety of goods on sale was amazing. A long counter ran along one side and Sam noticed heavy leather riding boots with price tags at one end. At the other end, strings of onions dangled down from the ceiling. A bunch of uniformed guardsmen laughed and joked together over a meal of roast beef and greens, their swords and helmets stacked neatly beside them. Their wine glasses were full and empty bottles lay scattered across the massive oak table. At the far end stood a mixed group of soldiers and civilians deep in conversation. Sam saw Mary Seacole threading her way through the throng towards them and so he followed.

'Sam, I'd like you to meet one or two of my

friends,' Mary smiled as the boy joined them. 'This gentleman is Mr William Howard Russell of *The Times*. He's here to tell the folks back home all about the war. And he doesn't always make himself popular with the politicians or the generals here in the Crimea. They call his paper 'The Thunderer' and his reports certainly make loud noises, I can tell you.'

The newspaperman, stocky and strong looking with an alert, intelligent face and a bushy beard, took a pipe out of his mouth and smiled at Sam.

'Billy here, not popular with the generals, Mary? I'm a general and he's popular with me, my dear. He's done a lot of good; it's important for people to know we've lost more men through disease than in battle.' The speaker was a tall, soldierly man, dressed in full uniform. He spoke with a slight Scots burr and Sam guessed him to be in his late thirties or early forties.

'This is Sir John Campbell,' Sam heard Mary say. 'Tell him in your own words about the ambush.' Sam was overwhelmed at the thought that this tall, fine-looking soldier was now involved, and began to feel his father was in safe hands.

Quickly he related what he, Ishmael and Mireli had heard in the church, their flight from Sebastopol, his capture by the bandits, his escape and coming across Mary near Inkerman.

Chapter 7

The Ambush

The General looked thoughtful for a few moments and then asked a question. 'And you say the ambush is to be somewhere near the village of Kadikoi but you don't know exactly where?'

'No, sir.'

'Then we'll have to take a chance,' replied Sir John in clipped tones. He reached into his back pocket and fished out a scrap of paper. Mary handed him a pencil and the others craned their necks as he sketched out a map of the area. 'Balaclava, as we all know, is at sea level and the land rises from there to a plateau at Kadikoi. By the time the wagon reaches the top of the slope the horses will be tired and so they'll be slow. The soldiers are likely to be concentrating their efforts on reaching the plateau and won't be too vigilant. That's where we'll assume the ambush will be, at the brow of the hill.' He jabbed a finger at a cross marked on the map and turned to a sergeant drinking with friends at the long table. 'Sergeant Napier, I want you to round up twenty of our best men and be sure they have their rifles and sabres. Have them here in half an hour. At the double man, there's no time to lose.' The sergeant and his companions abandoned their drinks and immediately left the Hotel.

'Now, Sam,' said the General, 'we'll take care of things at this end. There'll be a detachment of soldiers ready for the scoundrels if they dare show their faces. Mary will find you dry clothes, then make your way, as quickly as possible, down to Balaclava Harbour where your father will be helping unload the money from the ship. Warn him about the ambush and tell him, from me, to conceal as many of his men as possible on the wagon. Tell him not to delay, though, we don't want to raise the suspicions of these brutes or they might not attack. Then they'll hang around in the hills till the war's over, planning fresh mischief. We need to deal with their villainy now. Make an end of 'em for good.' By the end of his speech the normally calm Sir John was red faced with anger.

Half an hour later, Carrots with Sam on his back was ambling along the dockside at Balaclava looking for Colonel Hopwood. It was slow going because the countless groups of soldiers, sailors and civilians made identification of the escort difficult. As usual the number of ships loading and unloading was immense. The best were owned by the Royal Navy. This was not surprising since it was naval activity that gave the Allies a decisive advantage over the Russians in the Crimean War. No ship, Russian or otherwise, was even allowed to cross the Black Sea without the permission of the Royal Navy. Finally Sam decided to wait by the exit road, as his father and the men had no option but to pass that way.

He wasn't there long before Captain Hopwood appeared on horseback, threading his way through the crush followed by a large, covered ox cart. Bringing up the rear were six mounted escorts dressed in the uniform of the 11th

Hussars. Quickly the boy described his adventures in Sebastopol, the scheme for the ambush and Sir John's plans. Captain Hopwood pondered for a moment, called his troop to order and then made an announcement.

'There's been a change of plan I'm afraid. Apparently we may be ambushed at the top of the hill near Kadikoi and here's what we do. Davis, Sutherland, West and Lewis you're to conceal yourselves under the cover but keep your sabres in your hands. Harrison and Douglas take your horses back to Balaclava and ask for four volunteers. It shouldn't be difficult, they'll be glad of a rest from unloading that confounded ship. And they'll be eager to exercise their sword arms. Then catch us up and fall in behind. We'll have our own little surprise for these gentlemen.' He patted Sam on the head and gave him a fatherly smile. 'And you, son, will have to come with us. If you try to get back to Kadikoi you'll be seen and Ivan is bound to smell a rat. So hop in under the cover and don't come out when the ambush starts. This is a job for soldiers, not a boy. Carrots will be tethered behind the wagon.'

Near the top of the slope, just before the village, the road had been cut through the rock leaving sheer cliffs to either side. These were now overgrown with long grass and wiry shrubs. Sir John Campbell had marked this as the likely place for Ivan's trap and Sam took the opportunity to peep out as they passed the spot. Nothing happened and by the time they reached the end of the cliffs he was beginning to think Sir John was wrong. Then he noticed a man trotting soundlessly by the side of the wagon. Their eyes met and Sam saw the look of shocked surprise on his face. Sam was too dismayed to respond at first but then he found his voice and began to yell. Completely forgetting his father's order to stay hidden he jumped to his feet, pushing back the heavy canvas cover.

The sight before him caused him to shake his head in disbelief. They were under attack by a mob of at least fifty armed ruffians moving silently and at great speed towards them. Most were dressed in coarse woollen jerkins with green or grey breeches used as camouflage. Many carried cudgels, crudely cut from thick branches. Others wore cutlasses, probably Royal Navy issue and some brandished long daggers. This was no half-hearted assault by a bunch of novices but a well-planned operation that would have done credit to the Royal Marines. And the four soldiers with him on the wagon were only now struggling to their feet, while the six escorts had just noticed the danger and were spurring their mounts forward. Colonel Hopwood, taken by surprise, was in the act of turning his horse round.

The attackers were now yelling and screaming to create panic among the defenders. The strange mixture of hard-faced hill bandits and deserters was made more fearsome by the streaks of mud smeared across their features. The man who had first approached swung his cudgel at Sam's head and the boy ducked, feeling its breeze against his cheek.

'English pig,' snarled the ruffian as he clambered aboard, grappling with the boy for support. Sam's knees buckled and the breath left his body; his attacker was too strong. Suddenly the pressure round his waist eased. With a loud groan, the man staggered back clutching his head, then turned before crashing heavily back onto the road.

Sergeant West brandished his rifle butt and smiled grimly in Sam's direction. A French deserter in a tattered uniform jumped up and Sutherland wrestled him off but it was no use. Three more took his place and others were struggling to get on. The sheer weight of numbers was beginning to tell. The mounted escort were in the thick of the throng, slashing about them with their sabres. He heard his father shouting to him, something like 'get down' but he knew there was no point. The fighting was hand to hand and the soldiers had no chance to use their rifles. They were being overwhelmed, the end couldn't be long delayed and within minutes the army's cash would be in the hands of criminals.

From the corner of his eye Sam caught sight of Razor George being lifted bodily by Corporal Sutherland and thrown into the ranks of his cronies. The boy gained a certain gloomy satisfaction in seeing his adversary grovelling in the dust, gasping for breath.

Sam felt the wagon roll forward and saw Ivan astride the ox's back urging the great beast forward, while other bandits heaved on the shafts. Soon they'd be away from the spot and he'd be a prisoner again. He leaned over and untied Carrots. No sense in them both being captured. Then came the sound of a distant bugle from the direction of Kadikoi.

Almost to a man the brigands recognised the sound and melted away into the countryside they knew so well. Ivan from his position on the ox turned and bellowed an order in Russian but it fell on deaf ears. Hooves clattered as a detachment of cavalry in military formation with Sir John Campbell at its head appeared round the bend in the road. The sight of drawn sabres sent the remaining bandits clambering up the cliffs. Ivan was in the lead, closely followed by Razor, and they were almost at the top before the soldiers had time to respond.

Sam bounded from the wagon, leapt at the

embankment and gained a hold on a jutting bush. Then, agile as a monkey, he scrambled upwards, his light body and strong arms now giving him the advantage. The much heavier Ivan was clumsy by comparison and still in pain from his ribs. This slowed him down enough for the boy to grasp a leather boot just as it was vanishing over the cliff edge. Sam held firm with both arms, forcing the weakened bandit leader to bear the combined weight of both their bodies. It was too much and they tumbled, rolling over and over down the slope, dislodging clods of earth as they went.

Ivan was underneath at the bottom, so breaking Sam's fall. The man gasped in pain but, incredibly, still had the strength to shove the boy to one side. Then he was on his knees, staggering to his feet and snarling like an animal. Sam was rooted to the spot, staring at the dagger, uncertain how to react. He didn't even know if Ivan still had the strength to use the knife he had drawn.

In the event, action on his part was unnecessary. There was a blur of brown fur as the flashing hooves of Carrot's hind legs struck Ivan in the ribs, exactly as before. The man toppled like a forest tree in a gale then lay motionless as Carrots raised his head to the sky and eeyored in triumph. Sam went over and looked down at his unconscious enemy. How strange it was to think the helpless man had once inspired so much fear.

The celebrations continued till late in the evening at the British Hotel. Colonel Hopwood and Sir John Campbell got on famously as they ate and drank together and swapped yarns. Mary kept them and both groups of cavalrymen supplied with drinks and sampled quite a few herself. Carrots was in the stable at the back, munching his way through a huge sack of carrots that Mary had taken from her stores.

'Fresh in by boat from Southampton this mornin',' she'd said. 'Fetched them from Balaclava Harbour myself.'

'Thank you, Aunty Seacole,' said Sam. 'They should keep him going for a day or so.'

Mary recoiled in horror. 'A day or so, mercy me! I thought there was a month's supply there, at least.'

By the end of the evening Mary had offered Sam a job in the Hotel and Colonel Hopwood had agreed, taking it upon himself to let the Royal Artillery know what was happening.

'A good day's work, Hopwood,' said Sir John Campbell as he turned to leave. 'We'll hand the bandits over to the Russians at the next prisoner exchange and deal with the deserters ourselves. A pity we didn't get that scoundrel Razor George, though.'

He half opened the door and Sam heard a whistle outside. It was the signal he had heard from the hideout the previous night. He rushed out but saw only shadows vanish into the darkness. And there, tethered firmly to the rail outside, were a furious Razor George and the French deserter, who looked decidedly sorry for himself. The Romanies had disposed of their last enemies.

The next morning Sam rose early and started work in the shop. By noon he had sold groceries, served a meal to a group of naval officers and fed the animals. These included the chickens, which were being bred for slaughter, the horses, Mary's pack mules and Carrots. It was a freezing winter's day and snow had fallen heavily during the night. Sam had slept little while the blizzard raged and still felt cold as he went about his tasks, so he asked Mary if the British Hotel stocked warm clothing.

'Take it out of my wages, Aunty Seacole; I don't want something for nothing,' said the boy.

'I noticed your teeth chatterin'. You're not feeling sick or anythin' are you?' Mary sounded concerned for the well being of her assistant.

'I just can't seem to get warm. I've experienced cold weather before, 'cos I slept under a bridge with just a tarpaulin for cover after my dad died, my first dad that is, but that was London. This is Russia and it seems much colder.'

Mary walked to the back of the shop and peered

at a stack of large wooden trunks. 'I think I may have the very thing for you and you won't have to pay. The ladies back in Britain have been doin' some knittin' for charity and these garments have been shipped in from England. Let me see now. Ah, this was the one.' She reached up and pulled down a heavy box without any apparent effort and then began rummaging through the contents. 'Yes, here you are, these new helmets should keep your ears warm at least.'

Sam began pulling the tight-fitting woolly over his head, and found it surprisingly difficult. After several minutes of struggle he still had one eye covered by the thick material and it hadn't pulled down properly over his chin. His ear was twisted and felt as if it was about to be torn loose. Mary glanced up and smiled, then gave a broad grin and finally, losing control, collapsed into helpless laughter. 'Oh, Sam, you'll be the death of me, you really will. You remind me of the drunks in my sister's bar back in Jamaica. Half of 'em can't get their coats on straight at chuckin'-out time.'

She stood him in front of a mirror and after a long struggle, managed to straighten it after a fashion. 'Do you know what they're calling them, the ladies who do the knittin'?' Sam shook his head. 'Balaclava helmets; and I'll tell you something else, I've got some woollen jackets which button at the front.'

'And what are those called?' said Sam, his curiosity aroused.

'Cardigans, named after that old fool Lord Cardigan and him responsible for the deaths of all those good boys in the Light Brigade. Trouble is, he's a hero back home now after Lord Tennyson wrote that poem about the Charge and he's even been to meet the Queen.' And so it was that in the fierce winter cold of 1855 Sam set about his work in one of the first Balaclava helmets and one of the first Cardigans.

Disease among the soldiers of the Crimea was a greater danger than enemy gunfire and many of the sick visited Mary Seacole for help. She kept a stock of medicines and pills which could cure anything from jaundice to dysentery and a constant queue of patients waited for treatment.

The Russians shelled the British and French lines on most days and Mary went out to tend the wounded. When the firing was heavy she got Sam to fill several panniers with medicines and bandages and put them on the pack mules. Then he led the mules out to where the casualties were and helped her tend the injured. The fact is that the women taken on by the army as nurses were not allowed near the battle front. They were forced to work in Scutari over three hundred miles away, on the other side of the Black Sea. Even Florence Nightingale was restricted in this way, although she had been escorted around the army hospitals in the Crimea. That left only Mary Seacole, who was listed simply as a hotel keeper, as the only nurse that wounded and sick soldiers could turn to for immediate help. Everyone knew that many died on the journey before they reached the hospital at Scutari.

It was dangerous work in reach of the enemy guns and once, when Sam was with her, a shell whistled low overhead. Someone shouted, 'Lie down mother, lie down.' She and Sam threw themselves to the ground and a shot ploughed the ground near where they'd been standing.

Much of Mary's time was taken up with visiting the sick in their tents,and she nursed one young man through a long period of illness. One day when Sam had been visiting his father he returned to find her crying bitterly and he knew the man had gone beyond all need of nursing.

'He had fair hair and blue eyes, just like you Sam, and I helped him get better,' Mary said between sobs. 'Then he got out of bed and went back to his gun. He was in the Royal Artillery, you know. You may even have seen him when you worked on the ambulances. Anyway, a shell hit him and when I got there, his yellow hair was all stiff and stained with blood. Then just before he died he asked me to write to his mother and sister. She's a widow and he was her only son.' Mary

Seacole burst into tears once again and Sam could only put his hand on her shoulder and look on helplessly.

Slowly winter gave way to spring and still Sebastopol had not fallen to the Allies. By June the British and French commanders were desperate and one hot summer's day they ordered an all-out attack on the city. It failed and thousands of soldiers were injured or killed. Among the dead was their friend Sir John Campbell. For a long time Mary was heartbroken and only her sense of duty kept her working. 'I've known Sir John and Lady Campbell since they stayed at my home in Jamaica. Sir John was stationed there, you know,' she confided in Sam.

Mary was an early riser who was usually out of bed by four o'clock, cutting meat, then mixing medicines. By about seven Sam was up giving her a hand serving coffee to the Army Works Corps, the builders of the military road to the battlefront. Then Mary and Sam had an hour to get breakfast ready for the rush at nine o'clock. And so it went on all day, unless there were casualties to deal with. Mary Seacole was a stockily built woman who seemed to have boundless strength and energy. Just watching her in action made him feel tired.

'How do you manage to keep working at this pace the whole time? Don't you ever get exhausted?' he asked her late one evening.

'Well, Sam, to tell you the truth I don't rightly know. One thing's for sure, the good Lord gave me a strong constitution and I pray for strength the whole time. But I'm a lot more fatigued now than I was a few weeks back and at the moment I'm just hangin' on waitin' for the war to end. If it doesn't come soon, my health could well be broken for good.'

'I think we both ought to pray for your health every day,' said Sam. 'Rob Roy Macgregor of the Ragged School Union taught all of us trainee shoe blacks to pray every day while he was teaching us to be shoe blacks. My prayers were answered and I got new parents to look after me when the old ones died. So, I've been praying ever since.' And so the former waif from the streets of London and the nurse from Jamaica knelt to pray that God would keep her fit and healthy to allow her to continue in her work. The prayers were answered, too, because she carried on serving the sick and wounded until the end of the Crimean War.

Sometimes a customer would abuse Mary because of her dark skin and she'd become very upset. 'I got this kind of talk from the Yankees when I was in Panama but I never expected it from the British.' Once, before the attack on Sebastopol, a drunken sergeant made the mistake of jeering at her and calling her names in front of

Sir John Campbell. Without hesitation, the Major-General strode across the room and reprimanded him so severely, right in front of his men, that he never came back.

In August the Russians attacked for the last time. On this occasion they crossed the Chernaya River, near where Sam's boat had capsized, only to be beaten back by Allied gunfire. The Battle of Chernaya didn't last long and British troops were not even involved. Afterwards Mary helped attend to some injured Russians. One handsome young officer, mortally wounded, gave her his ring in gratitude for her care and then kissed her hand as she helped him on to the ambulance. A few minutes later he was dead.

Encouraged by the feebleness of the Russian attack on the Chernaya, the Allies made fresh plans and attacked Sebastopol with great determination, a month later, in September. This time they broke through the walls and took the city.

Chapter 8

Homeward Bound

The following morning, a Sunday, Mary Seacole with her pack mules, Colonel Hopwood on his charger and Sam on Carrots entered the stricken city. Mary's presence was noted by William Russell of *The Times* who mentioned her in his article. 'I saw her at the fall of Sebastopol, laden not with plunder, good old soul! But with wine, bandages, and food for the wounded or the prisoners.'

During the night the Russians had started fires which could be seen as far away as the heights of Balaclava. These continued well into the next day and were as much a danger to the victorious Allied troops as to the townspeople. The little church, where Sam had witnessed Ivan and George hatching their plots, was a smouldering ruin. Conditions in the town were very bad with Allied soldiers out of control and searching for plunder. Some had looted cellars for wine and were roaring drunk. Others had taken liquor from bars. A bunch of tipsy hussars wearing women's dresses and bonnets were lurching along the street, slurring the words of a barrack room ballad.

Many on guard duty had not eaten for hours and Mary stopped to serve them refreshments. Afterwards, at her request, the three of them visited the hospital, where thousands of dead and injured soldiers had been left behind when the Russians retreated. British and French Army doctors were already examining the survivors but the outlook was not bright. One young surgeon told them the wounded were too far gone and that nearly all would die within forty-eight hours. He also warned them to beware of exploding booby traps, which had been left to harm the occupying army. A Royal Marine had already lost a hand picking one up and several others had been badly hurt.

At Mary's suggestion she and Sam stayed for a time to help tend the wounded. They went from patient to patient, praying over each one and then Mary used her nursing skills to apply bandages or give doses of her herbal medicines. In some cases all they could do was to tell doctors that an operation was needed.

'I think the young surgeon was right, most of these young men are going to die anyway,' said Mary. 'But we've prayed and I'm sure that God will work some miracles. Later, when their work was complete, Colonel Hopwood returned and the three continued their journey.

They moved on to the north side of the harbour and were warned by a sentry to be careful as the enemy was firing from the other side of Inkerman Bay. 'See, Sam, over there. That's how the Russians got away from us,' said Colonel Hopwood pointing excitedly out to sea.

The boy gave a whistle of surprise. 'It looks like a bridge made out of boats,' he said.

'That's exactly what it is. They took weeks to build it and we all thought it was to bring reinforcements in, but we were wrong. When they knew Sebastopol was going to fall they set fire to the place and then the whole army retreated over it,' explained Colonel Hopwood.

'So what's happened? Have we won the war or not?' said Sam.

'A good question, son. The enemy went to the fortress across the bay. You can just about see it from here. It's a place called Severnaya and that's where all the shells are coming from. And there's the problem. Although we've destroyed their navy, the army is still intact. Personally, I can't see them coming to the negotiating table in a hurry,' replied his father.

The shelling intensified and one whistled in towards where they were standing. Sam and Mary threw themselves to the ground leaving the Colonel standing, unmoving and unflinching. The shell exploded harmlessly in a street behind them. Laughing, he helped first Mary and then Sam to their feet.

'You've got a bit of growing up to do before you're fit to join the army my boy,' he smiled as he clapped a fatherly hand to Sam's shoulder. 'Just as well Lord Cardigan wasn't here to see you rolling around in the gutter. He'd have had you court-martialled.'

A few weeks later Colonel Hopwood received a letter from London saying he'd been posted back to England. 'Say goodbye to your friends Sam, we're sailing on the next troopship,' he sighed. 'I know it's hard for you but we do need you at home.'

'That's only two days; it doesn't give me much time. I've got so many friends to see, Papa,' said the boy sadly.

The next morning he went up onto the heights to see Ishmael and Mireli but the Romany camp was deserted. The only signs of habitation were a huge patch of dead grass where the horses had been and the ashes of the fire. Apart from that there was nothing, not so much as a broken toy. There's no sign of a struggle, so I don't suppose they were cleared out by a Cossack patrol, mused Sam feeling relieved. They must have moved on to Transylvania or Hungary, one of those places that Ishmael spoke about. He was bitterly disappointed at the thought of never seeing his friend again but there was nothing he could do. The gypsies were a nomadic people who seldom stayed in one place for long. He wiped a tear from his eye and went back to the British Hotel.

The troopship left its moorings in Balaclava Harbour and moved slowly towards the narrow exit that led to the Black Sea and home. Mary Seacole in her best tartan dress waved frantically from the quayside. Suddenly Sam felt a deep sense of loss and an overwhelming sadness. After months away, he now knew places like Balaclava,

Kadikoi and Sebastopol as well as he knew London.

And there were the friends he had made in the Crimea. Most of them he would never see again, he knew that. By this time next year many of his army friends would be on long tours of duty in faraway places he'd never heard of and was never likely to visit. Joe was different, he lived in a little house in Wapping, just along the Thames from Blackwall, and Carrots could have him there in a quarter of an hour.

They were leaving Balaclava behind now and Sam turned to look back for the last time. The harbour looked so beautiful, like an inland lake of vivid blue he'd once seen in a picture. The town itself, a collection of dolls' houses nestling in the steep green hills surrounding the water, suddenly seemed irresistible and he had a powerful yearning to stay there for the rest of his life.

Carrots, who the Captain was allowing to stay on deck until they were out of sight of land, suddenly looked up and started to bray furiously. His frantic eeyoring brought the ship's crew to the rail, where they followed the donkey's gaze. And there, lined up on the cliffs above, were the Romanies. In front and waving handkerchiefs were Ishmael and Mireli with Amos and Hannah. The others were lined up behind, banging out a rhythm on old tin lids and making a furious din.

Nearby the gaudy gypsy waggons were drawn into a circle.

Sam and Colonel Hopwood waved back to a chorus of yelling and whistling from the crew. The boy managed to catch the words 'goodbye English and good luck', as they were borne across by the wind and then they were out of earshot. The salt tears ran freely down Sam's face and trickled into the corners of his mouth. Ishmael had been a friend in need and would be sorely missed. Somehow he knew their paths would never cross again. His father put a comforting arm around him but said nothing. Then they both stared at the cliffs till they were out of sight.

'Come on son, let's get Carrots below,' said the Colonel at length. 'And the Captain's invited us to dinner. I expect he wants to hear about the Light Brigade,' he said with a sigh. The evening at the dinner went slowly for Sam but he did learn one thing. The Captain had the latest news from London and his father had been right about Russian thinking. They were refusing to come to the conference table. The war was not yet over.

As the ship docked in Southampton, Sam saw his mother and little Sophie waiting patiently. A joyful reunion followed as the family came together for the first time in over a year. Sam had been gone fourteen months, Colonel Hopwood a little longer.

'Sam, how you've grown,' were his mother's first words on seeing him. 'Quite the young man.'

'And Sophie, she's big too. She's not a baby any more, she's a little girl,' said Sam as he scooped his sister up into his arms and kissed her on both cheeks.

They stayed the night at a waterfront inn and then the next morning, Colonel Hopwood had to report to the military authorities. The arrangement was that Sam would take his mother and sister back to London by donkey cart, just as soon as his father bought him a new one. The journey would take several days and Colonel Hopwood would see them at home in Blackwall in about a week.

Sam lay awake in the bedroom in the family's cottage by the Thames. He'd tried to sleep but it was no good. He'd been home for a month but he was finding it difficult to settle. London seemed so peaceful after the uproar of the Crimea. There was no whistling of shells, no thunder of guns, just tranquility and the sounds of river traffic. Yet it was too quiet, he'd grown used to the presence of danger.

He got up and went to the window. Carrots was contentedly munching grass in the garden, his good ear flopping across his head. He went downstairs and entered the kitchen just as his father came in with the paper.

'Morning Sam, there's some excellent news in *The Times* this morning,' said Colonel Hopwood in cheerful tones.

'That's good, Papa,' said Sam. 'Is it about the Crimea?'

'Yes, the Russians have signed the peace treaty in Paris. The war is now officially over and the Allies have won,' continued his father.

'Strange they should sign now,' replied Sam, 'after holding out for so long. What happened to make them change their minds?'

'A good question my boy,' said Colonel Hopwood settling back into his armchair as he always did when he was in the mood for a chat. 'It was the Navy that turned the tide in the end. They gathered together a great fleet of iron-clad battleships and gunboats, which they called the "Great Armament". Then the government threatened the Russians. It said, "If you don't sign the peace treaty we will send our fleet into the Baltic Sea and attack Kronstadt." The Russians don't know how to make iron warships, you see, so they had no choice but to surrender. Wooden ships stand no chance against the modern Royal Navy.'

'But where's Kronstadt and what's so special about it,' said Sam in puzzled tones?

'Well, the Russian capital city is a place called St Petersburg. It's a beautiful place and perhaps we'll go there as a family some time. Anyway, it's in the Baltic Sea up past Denmark, and Kronstadt is an island just outside St Petersburg. It's the main Russian naval base and nearly all their fleet is there.'

'Not like Sebastopol with only a small fleet,' said Sam. 'And if we captured Kronstadt, St Petersburg would be open to attack.'

'Precisely, but I wish it had been the Army and not the Navy that decided things,' said the Colonel. 'My naval friends will be unbearable after this.'

Sam's mother bustled into the room with Sophie, who jumped up onto Sam's lap and snuggled down. 'Have you told him about our enquiries, my dear,' she said?

'I was just about to,' replied Colonel Hopwood smiling.

Sam looked from his father to his mother and back again and beamed expectantly. 'Have you got a surprise for me?' he said.

'Well Sam, your mother heard a rumour that the Hospital Conveyance Corps is to be re-formed so I've been looking into it. As you know from your own experience it wasn't very successful in the Crimea, mainly because it was done on the cheap.'

'They employed nearly all army pensioners,' said Sam.

'But now they want to do it properly, with

specially trained personnel,' continued his father. 'They're thinking of calling it the Army Medical Corps or something like that. Your mother and I thought you might be interested.'

Sam whooped with delight and hugged Sophie. Interested! That was putting it mildly; it was something he'd dreamed about since first putting on the grey uniform in the Crimea. It wasn't often that a former waif from the streets was given such an opportunity.

'I expect Miss Nightingale will recommend you and, of course, you have the experience,' said his mother. 'And what with your father's influence you should go in with a commission. There's no immediate hurry, it might take a year or so for the army to organise itself. That gives you time to improve your education.'

Sam took Sophie's hand and led her out into the garden. He felt good inside. Not only did he have a loving family but he had the chance to make something of his life. He lifted Sophie and she shyly put a carrot into the donkey's mouth. The grumpy look disappeared and Carrots, the warrior donkey,took the vegetable with such gentleness that his teeth never so much as brushed the little girl's hand. Sophie giggled happily and Sam smiled a smile of peace.